PROJECT AIR FORCE

Promoting Airmen with the Potential to Lead

A Study of the Air Force Master Sergeant Promotion System

Kirsten M. Keller, Sean Robson, Kevin O'Neill, Paul D. Emslie, Lane F. Burgette, Lisa M. Harrington, Dennis Curran

Prepared for the United States Air Force

Approved for public release; distribution unlimited

For more information on this publication, visit www.rand.org/t/RR581

Library of Congress Control Number: 2014954285

ISBN: 978-0-8330-8585-6

Support RAND
Make a tax-deductible charitable contribution at
www.rand.org/giving/contribute

www.rand.org

Preface

This report documents research examining the effectiveness of the Weighted Airman Promotion System (WAPS) in selecting airmen with the potential to be effective leaders as master sergeants. It describes the range of leadership knowledge, skills, abilities, and other characteristics that master sergeants need to perform well in the Air Force, and examines the extent to which these attributes are measured in WAPS. The report also includes recommendations, based on our findings, for improvements to the master sergeant promotion system.

The research reported here was commissioned by the Director, Force Development, Deputy Chief of Staff for Manpower and Personnel, Headquarters United States Air Force (HQ USAF/A1D) and was conducted within the Manpower, Personnel, and Training Program of RAND Project AIR FORCE as part of a fiscal year 2012 project, "Enhancing Force Management and Development." This report should be of interest to Air Force leadership and staff involved in the policy and execution of the enlisted promotion system.

RAND Project AIR FORCE

RAND Project AIR FORCE (PAF), a division of the RAND Corporation, is the U.S. Air Force's federally funded research and development center for studies and analyses. PAF provides the Air Force with independent analyses of policy alternatives affecting the development, employment, combat readiness, and support of current and future air, space, and cyber forces. Research is conducted in four programs: Force Modernization and Employment; Manpower, Personnel, and Training; Resource Management; and Strategy and Doctrine. The research reported here was prepared under contract FA7014-06-C-0001.

Additional information about PAF is available on our website:
http://www.rand.org/paf/

Contents

Figures

Tables

Summary

As operations become more jointly connected with other military services and the Air Force becomes smaller, there is concern that more leadership responsibility and authority is being pushed down to noncommissioned officers. Therefore, as the first level of senior noncommissioned officer leadership, the ability of master sergeants (E-7) to be effective leaders is especially critical. In addition to training and development efforts, a key component of ensuring that master sergeants have the knowledge, skills, abilities, and other characteristics (KSAOs) needed to fulfill the required leadership responsibilities is having an effective system to promote airmen with the greatest potential from the E-6 rank of technical sergeant to master sergeant. The current promotion system was developed more than 40 years ago and is designed to "identify those people with the highest potential to fill positions of increased grade and responsibility" (U.S. Air Force, 1993, p. 1). Despite changes in force size, operational requirements, and airmen's responsibilities, the Weighted Airman Promotion System (WAPS) and its underlying factors have remained largely unchanged since its establishment.

Therefore, the goal of this study was to examine the master sergeant promotion system and provide recommendations for improving it. Our work was driven by three primary research questions: (1) What are the KSAOs that master sergeants need to be good leaders? (2) Is the current system effective at promoting airmen with the KSAOs needed to be good leaders? (3) If necessary, what are potential options for improving the master sergeant promotion system to ensure that master sergeants have the KSAOs they need to succeed?

Analytical Approach

To address each of these questions, we gathered information from a variety of sources. To examine the KSAOs that master sergeants need to be good leaders, we conducted:

- a review of Air Force policy that outlines key responsibilities and competencies for each enlisted grade
- a review of prior research on general and military-specific leadership KSAOs
- interviews with two senior enlisted leader advisory bodies and a small sample of wing, group, and squadron commanders.

To evaluate the effectiveness of the current system at promoting airmen with the KSAOs needed to be good leaders as master sergeants, we conducted:

- interviews with representatives involved in the policy and execution of WAPS
- an examination of the extent to which the current WAPS factors measure the important leadership KSAOs identified in our review

- a statistical examination of the relative influence of each WAPS factor on promotion outcomes to determine how the current promotion system is actually functioning relative to its intended design.

Finally, we explored potential options for improving the master sergeant promotion system based on findings from our interviews and published research on well-established assessment methods that could measure leadership potential. We also reviewed information and conducted interviews with representatives from the Army, Marine Corps, and Navy regarding their enlisted promotion systems to use as a comparison.

Master Sergeant Leadership Responsibilities and Related Knowledge, Skills, and Abilities

Master sergeants represent the first level of senior enlisted leadership in the Air Force and are expected to transition from being "technical experts and first line supervisors to leaders of operational competence skilled at merging subordinates' talents, skills, and resources with other teams' functions to most effectively accomplish the mission" (U.S. Air Force, 2009a, p. 14). Consistent with this Air Force expectation, our interview participants identified technical task work as a key duty, but further highlighted the increased importance of various leadership duties at the master sergeant rank, including providing professional and developmental feedback to airmen, delegating tasks, providing feedback to senior officers, managing resources, and engaging in self-development. Furthermore, interview participants noted that many of these master sergeant leadership duties have increased in importance or scope over the years.

Findings from our interviews and our review of prior research on leadership KSAOs highlighted a number of different attributes that master sergeants must have to be good leaders and to be able to perform their duties effectively. For example, both identified the importance of key technical knowledge as well as four general categories of skills (i.e., cognitive skills, interpersonal skills, business/management skills, and strategic skills) that seem to be consistently identified as important for leader effectiveness. In addition, prior research as well as our interview participants identified other characteristics such as general cognitive ability, personality attributes, and motivation to lead as important for leader effectiveness. As master sergeants move from being technical experts into leadership roles, it is important that the KSAOs that are needed to fulfill the increased leadership responsibilities are measured as part of the promotion system.

Effectiveness of the Current Master Sergeant Promotion System

WAPS is the current tool used by the Air Force to select enlisted airmen for promotion. It was developed to provide a more transparent, objective, and fair system for selecting airmen to be promoted to the next higher grade, using weighted factors intended to measure key knowledge, experience, and performance that allow airmen to more easily assess their probability of promotion. Airmen eligible for promotion to master sergeant are selected using the same factors as airmen eligible for promotion to E-5 and E-6. They can earn a total of 460 possible points based on:

- a specialty knowledge test (100 points)
- a Promotion Fitness Exam (100 points)
- time in grade (60 points)
- time in service (40 points)
- decorations (25 points)
- enlisted performance report (EPR) ratings (135 points).

Promotion to E-8 and E-9 utilizes a different knowledge test and includes a promotion board score worth up to 450 points.

Our analysis found that these WAPS factors have the potential to be good measures of many of the key KSAOs identified as important for leadership as a master sergeant. Specifically, the specialty knowledge tests and Promotion Fitness Exam are intended to provide direct measures of important declarative knowledge. Time in service and time in grade likely provide some degree of indirect or proxy measure of knowledge and skills. The EPR and decorations scores have the potential to provide direct and indirect measures of key procedural knowledge and skills and motivation through an assessment of past performance.

However, findings from our interviews indicated concerns with the overall effectiveness of the current promotion system, with participants noting some gaps in the KSAOs of master sergeants who are now being promoted and problems with inflated performance scores. Consistent with our interview findings, we found that three out of the six WAPS factors account for the vast majority of variance in who gets promoted (83 percent of the median relative influence of who gets promoted across Air Force specialty codes [AFSCs]): the specialty knowledge test, Promotion Fitness Exam, and time in grade. Of particular note, the EPR factor, which is intended to measure job performance, has only a 2-percent median relative influence on actual promotions across AFSCs. We found that it has little influence because there is little variance in EPR scores compared to other factors; the mean EPR score for all airmen eligible for promotion to master sergeant is 134 out of 135 points. Thus, current promotion outcomes are largely based only on whether airmen have the necessary knowledge and tenure, but not if they are able to actually apply that knowledge or have the motivation to take on the increased leadership responsibilities that will come with being a master sergeant. Overall, the current promotion process is not effectively assessing the full range of KSAOs or leadership potential needed to successfully perform as a master sergeant in the Air Force.

Potential Options for Improvement

To better measure the KSAOs necessary for fulfilling the increased leadership responsibilities of a master sergeant in the Air Force, we explored several potential options. The most obvious option is to revise the EPR to try to better differentiate among technical sergeant potential as a master sergeant. However, data on EPR scores over the last several decades suggest this is a longstanding issue that is deeply embedded in Air Force culture, making it potentially difficult to fully eliminate. Another avenue for addressing the gap in the current promotion system is to include additional factors in WAPS to better measure leadership potential as a master sergeant.

We examined some of the most widely researched methods available for selecting and promoting job candidates (i.e., personality inventories, biodata, structured interviews, assessment centers, work samples, situational judgment tests), including a board process that is commonly used in the military. Our selection, although not comprehensive, was guided by expert knowledge of available methods for personnel selection and promotion. Consequently, we did not review assessment methods found to be poor predictors of performance or that would fail to provide any incremental value to the current promotion system. We evaluated the trade-offs of these different methods to assess which might be best suited to improving the current promotion system's ability to select airmen who will be able to fulfill the increased leadership responsibilities of a master sergeant in the Air Force, while at the same time weighing other factors important to the Air Force in implementing any changes. In evaluating each assessment method, we used the following criteria:

- measurement of attributes: the extent to which the assessment method is able to assess a range of leadership attributes (i.e., KSAOs) relevant to predicting performance as a master sergeant in the Air Force
- validity: research evidence on the operational validity of each assessment method (i.e., typical relationship between the predictor and job performance)
- diversity: research evidence on the extent to which the assessment method may have an adverse impact on minority promotion[1]
- cost: additional cost to the Air Force to develop and/or implement the assessment method
- fairness perceptions: the extent to which airmen are likely to perceive the assessment method as a fair assessment of their potential.

Overall, we found that there are pros and cons to all of the assessment methods we evaluated. Based on our criteria, we found two methods particularly promising: (1) a situational judgment test, which is a multiple-choice test designed to measure the effectiveness of candidates'

---

[1] Adverse or disparate impact exists when an employment practice that is not intended to discriminate has an adverse effect on members of a particular race, ethnicity, religion, sex or national origin. For example, adverse impact would be said to exist when a particular promotion factor results in fewer women being promoted than men. A common rule of thumb for measuring the existence of adverse impact is the four-fifths rule, which says that adverse impact is considered present when an employment practice results in the proportion of applicants that are selected or promoted from a protected group, being less than four-fifths (80 percent) of the proportion of applicants selected or promoted from the group with the highest selection rate. For more information, see Equal Employment Opportunity Commission, 1978.

judgments about appropriate courses of action in response to different job-related problems or dilemmas, and (2) a promotion board, which has a panel of higher ranking airmen review and score the records of each eligible candidate (e.g., performance records, career history). Situational judgment tests are relatively inexpensive and can measure a broad range of KSAOs that existing WAPS factors do not assess. Although more expensive, the addition of a promotion board also has the potential to increase the breadth of KSAOs examined and may be able to better differentiate performance. From a fairness perspective, this is particularly important given that individuals expect their performance to be taken into account for promotion. Furthermore, the integration of a hurdle system as part of the board process, in which only a select percentage of candidates advance to the board based on an initial hurdle of having one of the top total WAPS scores, can reduce costs by requiring the board to review only a portion of candidates.

Recommendations

Based on the study findings, we developed the following recommendations:

Examine the validity and utility of implementing a situational judgment test and a master sergeant promotion board as additional measures of leadership potential. Based on our evaluation of additional measures that could be included in WAPS to better assess leadership potential as a master sergeant, a situational judgment test and promotion board seem particularly promising. However, we do not have data regarding the use of these assessment methods in the context of promoting Air Force technical sergeants to master sergeant and their potential relative contribution to WAPS. Therefore, consistent with *Principles of the Validation and Use of Personnel Selection Procedures* (Society for Industrial and Organizational Psychology, Inc., 2003), we recommend conducting a validation study with a sample of AFSCs to examine the validity of a board and situational judgment test as part of WAPS in terms of the criteria outlined previously (i.e., validity, diversity, and fairness), prior to their use in determining actual promotion outcomes. A validation study can also provide the evidence needed to evaluate the costs and benefits (i.e., utility) of including these additional measures in WAPS and help in determining appropriate weights for each factor (i.e., range of points assigned to each factor). Finally, such a study can examine and address any potential adverse impact on minorities or other issues, helping to ensure the new process will be accepted by airmen prior to full implementation.

Explore ways to improve the enlisted performance evaluation process using evidence-based practices. It was beyond the scope of this study to fully review the current enlisted evaluation process and EPRs, and it may be difficult to completely eliminate inflation of EPR scores given the immense cultural shift that would be required. However, we recommend that the Air Force explore potential improvements to the evaluation process in an effort to ensure that performance evaluations are as accurate as possible. Furthermore, a promotion board for master sergeants will only be as effective as the information they have to review. Therefore, it is critical that the EPR, which is the main source of information for the board, contain important and accurate information on performance that will be helpful in judging promotion potential. To this end, key principles in effective performance evaluation provide opportunities that the Air Force can explore regarding revising the EPR and overall evaluation process.

Continue to periodically reevaluate the effectiveness of the promotion system. Finally, we recommend that the Air Force continue to periodically reevaluate the effectiveness of the promotion system, not only for master sergeants, but for all enlisted ranks. As there are changes to the operational environment, force size, and responsibilities at each rank, it is critical to examine whether WAPS is effective at identifying airmen with the highest potential for promotion to the next grade. This evaluation should include examining the extent to which current promotion factors are measuring key KSAOs predictive of performance at the next rank and the predictive validity of WAPS as a whole.

In conclusion, although the current promotion system has the potential to measure many of the key KSAOs identified as important for leadership as a master sergeant, promotion outcomes are driven by knowledge tests and time in grade. Other skills and attributes that are important for successful performance as a master sergeant in the Air Force, including the motivation to lead, are not being assessed. Our research identified two additional assessment methods, a promotion board and situational judgment test, that we believe could help improve the effectiveness of the current promotion system.

Acknowledgements

We are grateful to the many people who were involved in this research. In particular, we would like to thank our U.S. Air Force sponsor, Mr. Russell Frasz, Director, Force Development, Office of the Deputy Chief of Staff for Manpower and Personnel (AF/A1D) as well as CMSAF James Roy and Brig Gen Gina Grosso (AF/A1P). We would especially like to thank our action officers for their help and guidance throughout this study: CMSgt Steve McDonald (AF/A1DI), CMSgt Nichols (AF/A1PPE), and CMSgt Ben Caro (AF/A1DI). We are also grateful for the information provided by personnel at the Air Force Personnel Center (AFPC) and the Board Secretariat regarding the implementation of the Weighted Airman Promotion System and promotion boards. Similarly, we are grateful to the various personnel from the Army, Navy, and Marine Corps who provided information to us regarding the policy and implementation of their service's enlisted promotion systems. In addition, we appreciate the time and candidness of the Air Force personnel who took time out of their busy schedules to participate in our interviews. This research would not have been possible without their contributions. This report also benefited from the helpful insights and comments provided by several RAND colleagues, including Michael Schiefer, Nelson Lim, Sarah Greathouse, Nolan Sweeney, Lindsay Daugherty, Albert Robbert, Chaitra Hardison, and Larry Hanser. Finally, we would like to thank Adele Palmer, Carra Sims, and Michael Thirtle, who provided reviews of this report. Their comments greatly contributed to improving the quality of this work.

Abbreviations

AFHRL	Air Force Human Resources Laboratory
AFOQT	Air Force Officer Qualifying Test
AFPC	Air Force Personnel Center
AFR	Air Force regulation
AFSC	Air Force specialty code
ALS	Airman Leadership School
APR	Airmen Performance Report
ARMS	Automated Records Management System
CCAF	Community College of the Air Force
CCS	chronic critical shortage
EBOD	Enlisted Board of Directors
eBOSS	Electronic Board Operations Support System
EFDP	Enlisted Force Development Panel
EPR	enlisted performance report
FTE	full-time-equivalent
GBM	generalized boosted model
HQ USAF	Headquarters U.S. Air Force
KSAO	knowledge, skills, abilities, and other characteristics
M&IE	meals and incidental expenses
MAJCOM	major command
NCO	noncommissioned officer
NCOA	Noncommissioned Officer Academy
PAF	Project AIR FORCE
PFE	Promotion Fitness Examination
PME	professional military education
SIOP	Society for Industrial and Organizational Psychology, Inc.
SJT	situational judgment test
SKT	specialty knowledge test
SNCO	senior noncommissioned officer

SNCOA	Senior Noncommissioned Officer Academy
TIG	time in grade
TIS	time in service
TOPCAP	Total Objective Plan for Career Airman Personnel
USAF	United States Air Force
USAFSE	United States Air Force Supervisory Exam
WAPS	Weighted Airman Promotion System

1. Introduction

Master sergeants hold the rank of E-7 and represent the first level of senior noncommissioned officers (SNCOs) in the U.S. Air Force (USAF). Upon attaining this rank, master sergeants are expected to transition from being "technical experts and first line supervisors to leaders of operational competence skilled at merging subordinates' talents, skills, and resources with other teams' functions to most effectively accomplish the mission" (USAF, 2009a, p. 14). As operations become more jointly connected with other military services and the Air Force becomes smaller, there is concern that more leadership responsibility and authority is being pushed down to noncommissioned officers (NCOs). Therefore, as the first level of senior enlisted leadership, the ability of master sergeants to be effective leaders is especially critical.

In addition to training and development efforts, a key component of ensuring that master sergeants have the required knowledge, skills, abilities, and other characteristics (KSAOs) to fulfill the required leadership responsibilities is having an effective system to promote airmen with the greatest potential from the E-6 rank of technical sergeant to master sergeant. The current promotion system, known as the Weighted Airman Promotion System (WAPS), was developed more than 40 years ago and is designed to "identify those people with the highest potential to fill positions of increased grade and responsibility" (USAF, 1993, p. 1). Despite changes in force size, operational requirements, and airmen's responsibilities, WAPS and its underlying factors have remained largely unchanged since its establishment. For these reasons, the Air Force Directorate of Force Development (AF/A1D) asked RAND Project AIR FORCE to examine the effectiveness of WAPS at selecting master sergeants able to fulfill the required leadership responsibilities.

Study Objective and Analytical Approach

The primary objective of this study was to examine the effectiveness of the master sergeant promotion system and provide recommendations for improving it. We are not able to empirically determine if WAPS is actually selecting the right airmen to be promoted to master sergeant, given that we do not have data on how well those individuals not selected for promotion to master sergeant might have performed. However, we can examine the extent to which WAPS is assessing key leadership KSAOs required to perform well as a master sergeant. Therefore, this study was driven by three primary research questions: (1) What are the KSAOs that master sergeants need to be good leaders? (2) Is the current system effective at promoting airmen with the KSAOs needed to be good leaders? (3) If necessary, what are potential options for improving the master sergeant promotion system to ensure master sergeants have the KSAOs they need to succeed?

1

To address each of these questions, we gathered information from a variety of sources. To examine the KSAOs that master sergeants need to be good leaders, we conducted:

- a review of Air Force policy that outlines key responsibilities and competencies for each enlisted grade
- a review of prior research on general and military-specific leadership KSAOs
- interviews with two senior enlisted leader advisory bodies and a small sample of wing, group, and squadron commanders.

To evaluate the effectiveness of the current system at promoting airmen with the KSAOs needed to be good leaders as master sergeants, we conducted:

- interviews with representatives involved in the policy and execution of WAPS
- an examination of the extent to which the current WAPS factors measure the important leadership KSAOs identified in our review
- a statistical examination of the relative influence of each WAPS factor on promotion outcomes to determine how the current promotion system is actually functioning relative to its intended design.

Finally, we explored potential options for improving the master sergeant promotion system based on findings from our interviews and published research on well-established assessment methods that could measure leadership potential. We also reviewed information and conducted interviews with representatives from the Army, Marine Corps, and Navy regarding their enlisted promotion systems to use as a comparison.

There are some limitations of this study that are important to note. First, conducting a full job analysis, a systematic technique for identifying job tasks and related knowledge, skills, and abilities, was beyond the scope of this study.[1] However, our interviews and review of the research literature highlight important KSAOs to be considered. Additionally, we were not able to evaluate all aspects of the enlisted promotion process in depth, such as the process for providing enlisted performance evaluations or the development of the tests included in WAPS. Finally, without more current data available, we treat the WAPS factor weights as indicators of current Air Force intentions regarding the relative influence each factor should have on promotion outcomes.

Organization of the Report

The remaining chapters in this report describe our research findings and recommendations. Chapter Two presents our findings on master sergeant leadership duties and the related leadership KSAOs that are important for performing well as a master sergeant in the Air Force. Chapters Three and Four provide an overview of WAPS and present our results on its

---

[1] See Brannick, Levine, and Morgeson (2007) for more information on job analysis methods.

effectiveness in selecting master sergeants who will be able to fulfill the required leadership responsibilities. Chapter Five follows with a discussion of options for improving WAPS. Finally, Chapter Six presents our conclusions and final recommendations.

The report also includes a number of appendixes. Appendix A provides examples of enlisted performance report forms. Appendix B describes our interview methodology and analysis. Appendix C provides descriptive statistics for scores on the WAPS factors. Appendix D presents a brief summary of the statistical analysis technique used to examine the relative influence of WAPS factors on promotion outcomes. Finally, Appendixes E and F provide greater details on the criteria we used to evaluate different assessment methods that could be used to improve WAPS.

2. Master Sergeant Leadership Responsibilities and Related Knowledge, Skills, and Abilities

Our first research question for this study focused on gaining a general understanding of the additional leadership responsibilities and duties of a master sergeant and related KSAOs that airmen may need to be able to fulfill these leadership responsibilities. In other words, what KSAOs are likely predictive of future performance (i.e., potential) as a master sergeant in the Air Force, and thus should be measured as part of the promotion system? To identify these attributes, we drew on Air Force policy that outlines key responsibilities and competencies for each enlisted grade, prior research on general and military-specific leadership KSAOs, and interviews with subject matter experts.

Master Sergeant Roles and Responsibilities

The USAF enlisted force is structured into three tiers of airmen that correspond to increasing levels of leadership responsibilities: (1) junior enlisted airmen, (2) NCOs, and (3) SNCOs (USAF, 2009a). Junior enlisted airmen (E-1 through E-4) are focused on "adapting to military requirements, achieving occupational proficiency, and learning how to be highly productive members of the Air Force" (USAF, 2009a, p. 4). NCOs (E-5 and E-6) are expected to focus on mission accomplishment and to "continue occupational growth and become expert technicians" (USAF, 2009a, p. 4). At the same time, they are expected to start developing as leaders, supervisors, and mentors in preparation for increased leadership responsibilities at the higher ranks. SNCOs (E-7 through E-9) also focus on mission accomplishment, but are expected to serve as leaders and supervisors for airmen at the lower ranks.

Master sergeants are the first level of senior enlisted leadership in the Air Force. Upon attaining the rank of E-7, master sergeants are expected to transition from being "technical experts and first line supervisors to leaders of operational competence skilled at merging subordinates' talents, skills, and resources with other teams' functions to most effectively accomplish the mission" (USAF, 2009a, p. 14).

To correspond with the different leadership responsibilities of each enlisted tier, the Air Force also outlines three leadership levels: tactical, operational, and strategic leadership (USAF, 2006). Junior enlisted airmen and NCOs are expected to function at the tactical level of leadership, while SNCOs are expected to function at the operational and strategic levels. Master sergeants, specifically, are expected to function at the operational leadership level. Senior master sergeants are expected to function at the operational or strategic leadership level, and chief master sergeants are expected to function at both the operational and strategic leadership levels.

As shown in Figure 2.1, each of these leadership levels varies in the extent to which different personal, people/team, and institutional leadership competencies are required (USAF, 2006). These competencies outline specific behaviors or demonstrated KSAOs expected at each leadership level. The specific KSAOs underlying these competencies will be discussed in the next section.

Figure 2.1. Air Force Leadership Levels

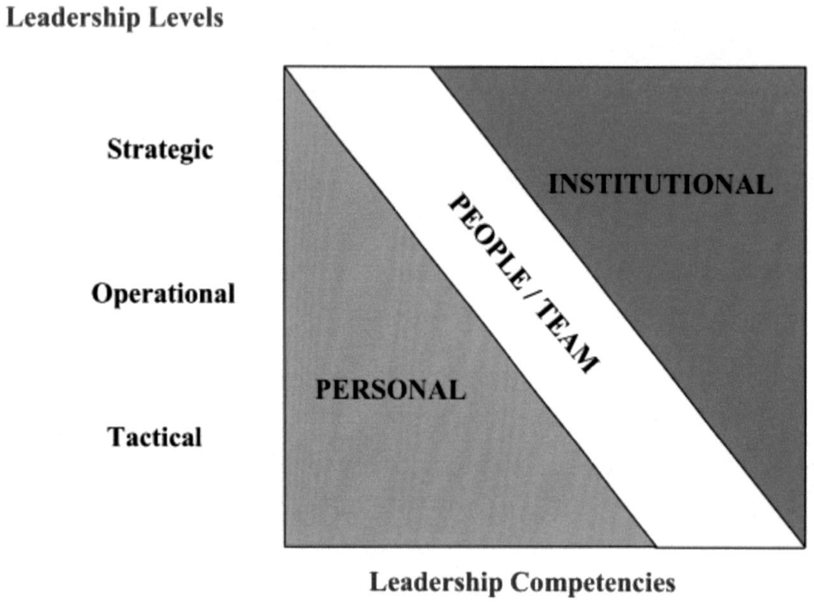

SOURCE: USAF, 2006.

Based on the leadership construct model displayed in Figure 2.1, operating at the tactical level of leadership places greater emphasis on personal leadership competencies than on people/team and institutional leadership competencies. The operational leadership level places equal emphasis on the personal, people/ team, and institutional leadership competencies. Finally, the strategic level places greater emphasis on institutional leadership competencies relative to the personal and people/team leadership competencies.

Table 2.1 outlines the specific components of each of these competencies. At the operational leadership level, master sergeants are expected to have roughly equal levels of the personal, people/ team, and institutional leadership competencies shown in Table 2.1 as their "leadership tasks become more complex and sophisticated" (USAF, 2006, p. 8).

Table 2.1. Leadership Competencies

Competency	Competency Components
Personal Leadership	• Exercise sound judgment • Adapt and perform under pressure • Inspire trust • Lead courageously • Assess self • Foster effective communications
People/Team Leadership	• Drive performance through shared visions, values, and accountability • Influence through win/win solutions • Mentor and coach for growth and success • Promote collaboration and teamwork • Partner to maximize results
Institutional Leadership	• Shape Air Force strategy and direction • Command organizational and mission success through enterprise integration and resource stewardship • Embrace change and transformation • Drive execution • Attract, retain, and develop talent

SOURCE: USAF, 2006.

Interview Findings

To gather additional information on the specific leadership responsibilities and duties of a master sergeant in the Air Force, we also conducted interviews with members of two senior enlisted leader advisory bodies: (1) the Enlisted Force Development Panel (EFDP), which is composed of chief master sergeants focused on effective development and utilization of the enlisted force; and (2) the Enlisted Board of Directors (EBOD), which is composed of the major commands (MAJCOM) command chiefs and enlisted leaders serving in other strategic positions (25 chief master sergeants total). To complement this SNCO perspective, we also conducted interviews with a small sample of wing, group, and squadron commanders representative of different Air Force bases and mission types (16 officers total, ranging in rank from lieutenant colonel to major general).[1]

---

[1] See Appendix B for details on the methodology and analysis of the interviews. Although we sought to gather information from key enlisted advisory bodies and Air Force officers to gain a more strategic perspective regarding the desired leadership responsibilities and duties of a master sergeant, similar data obtained directly from airmen holding the master sergeant rank may help provide a more detailed picture of job tasks—but this was beyond the scope of our study. As an alternative data source for the master sergeant perspective, we examined occupational analysis data for a very small cross-section of Air Force specialty codes (AFSCs) to ensure that we were not missing key supervisory or management tasks performed by master sergeants. Occupational analysis data are collected by the Occupational Analysis Division located under Air Education and Training Command. The division collects data on the specific tasks performed in each Air Force specialty on a three-year cycle, including general supervisory and management tasks. We examined occupational analysis data for a sample of ten different AFSCs drawn from different functional areas (e.g., loadmaster, pararescue, health services) to try to examine supervisory and

Consistent with the Air Force–designated responsibilities of a master sergeant already outlined, interview participants identified key duties that master sergeants are expected to perform that generally fell into the five following areas:

- completing technical task work
- leading and managing teams
- serving as a member of the leadership team
- managing resources
- engaging in self-development.

Our interview participants also noted that these master sergeant responsibilities have increased over the years, including an increase in the scope of expected leadership and supervisory duties, a greater focus on taking care of airmen, and increased expectations for participating in community events and advancing one's education. Furthermore, some master sergeants are now filling roles previously held by higher enlisted grades or junior officers (mentioned by 31 percent of participants).

In the following sections, we briefly define each of these responsibilities and describe the proportion of interview participants who mentioned each responsibility area. It is important to note, however, that these proportions represent responses to open-ended questions (such as, what are the most important leadership responsibilities of a master sergeant?). Therefore, the proportions should not be interpreted as the relative importance of responsibilities since interview participants generally relied upon memory to respond to these open-ended questions.

Completing Technical Task Work

As described previously, master sergeants are expected to be transitioning from being "technical experts . . . to leaders of operational competence." (USAF, 2009a, p. 14.) Consistent with this designation, 90 percent of our interview participants stated that one of the key duties of a master sergeant is still to carry out technical or functional work related to his or her specific career field.

Leading and Managing Teams

Consistent with the expectation that master sergeants will now take on a leadership role, the responsibility of leading and managing a team was mentioned by 82 percent of interview participants. Specific duties related to this area include providing developmental feedback,

---

management tasks that may be consistent for master sergeants across different types of AFSCs. Using the occupational analysis data, we identified specific supervisory and management tasks that were reported as being performed by airmen at the 7-skill level. Because performance of specific tasks was not broken out by pay grade, but was broken out by skill level, we focused on the highest skill level provided (7–skill level). Of course, this also included responses for technical sergeants (E-6) and some staff sergeants (E-5) who achieved a 7-skill level. Overall, we found that the duties described in our interviews were generally consistent with supervisory and management tasks identified in the occupational analysis surveys.

delegating task assignments, and taking care of airmen by monitoring and addressing any work group or personal issues that arise in the unit. The full list of duties in this area is provided in Table 2.2, along with the percentage of interview participants who identified the duty as a key master sergeant responsibility.

Table 2.2. Duties Related to Leading and Managing a Team

Duty	Description	Percentage of Participants Identifying Duty
Provide professional/ developmental feedback	Provide mentoring/coaching; provide guidance to airmen on training and education/PME needs and future assignments	85
Provide supervision/ performance feedback	Supervise task/technical area performance; provide performance feedback to subordinates	67
Taking care of airmen	Engage and get to know airmen; monitor any issues that arise in unit, such as low morale and personal/family problems	64
Provide task assignments/ delegation	Delegate tasks to subordinates; provide direction and guidance on work responsibilities to ensure mission accomplishment; help prioritize airmen tasks	56
Ensure mission execution	Ensure mission execution; ensure the job gets done	51
Discipline	Hold subordinates accountable by providing discipline/punishment	36
Lead by example	Maintain physical fitness standards, follow Air Force rules, model Air Force core values	33
Communicate broader mission	Help airmen connect their individual roles to broader wing and Air Force mission; provide a broader, longer-term perspective to unit mission	26
Motivate airmen	Motivate airmen to perform and execute the mission	26
Write performance reviews	Write enlisted performance reports (EPRs) and various performance-related articles, such as award recommendations	26
Manage risk/safety	Ensure that proper safety protocols (e.g., checklists) are followed; mange the potential for risk or errors within work unit	18

NOTE: *N* = 41; we only include duties identified by at least 10 percent of participants.

Serving as a Member of the Leadership Team

Interview participants also identified master sergeants as playing a key role in the overall leadership of a wing, group, or squadron. Specific duties related to this area and the percentage of interview participants who identified the duty as a key master sergeant responsibility are provided in Table 2.3. Not surprisingly, duties related to a master sergeant serving as a member of the leadership team were mentioned considerably more often by wing, group, and squadron commanders. Sixty-four percent of the officers we interviewed (compared to only 48 percent of SNCOs) identified a key duty of master sergeants as communicating senior leadership decisions to the enlisted force, and 79 percent of officers (compared to only 36 percent of SNCOs) identified a key duty of master sergeants as providing feedback to senior leaders on the state of the enlisted force. Thus, this difference may further highlight the increasing expectations that officers have for master sergeants.

Table 2.3. Duties Related to Serving as a Member of the Leadership Team

Duty	Description	Percentage of Participants Identifying Duty
Communicate senior leader decisions to enlisted corps	Communicate decisions, strategy, and instructions from senior leaders down to the enlisted corps level; translate higher-level communications from senior leaders down to specific tasks and directions for the enlisted corps	54
Provide feedback to senior leaders	Provide feedback to senior leaders on state of the enlisted corps (e.g., morale issues); provide feedback on senior leader decisions or strategy (i.e., report disagreement with course of action)	51
Provide guidance to company-grade officers	Provide guidance to company-grade officers on various unit issues, leadership, roles, and responsibilities	13

NOTE: *N* = 41; we only include duties identified by at least 10 percent of participants.

Managing Resources

Fifty-one percent of our interview participants also stated that another key duty of a master sergeant involved managing various resources, such as manpower, budgets, and equipment to ensure they were able to accomplish the mission as well as managing airmen's schedules and training plans.

Engaging in Self-Development

Finally, our interview participants stated that they expected master sergeants to be proactive and engage in additional activities to further their self-development. Specifically, participants stated that they expect good master sergeants to show leadership throughout their professional and nonprofessional lives, such as by volunteering as leaders in professional organizations, base activities, clubs, or wider community organizations (mentioned by 44 percent of participants). Similarly, participants stated that they expect a master sergeant to have not only completed the required professional military education (PME), but to have engaged in further professional development, such as getting a bachelor's or master's degree (mentioned by 21 percent of participants).

In summary, master sergeants represent the first level of enlisted senior leadership and are expected to transition from their technical responsibilities to demonstrating leadership. Consistent with this Air Force expectation, our interview participants identified technical task work as a key duty, but further highlighted the increased importance of various leadership duties at the master sergeant rank, including providing professional and developmental feedback to airmen, delegating tasks, providing feedback to senior officers, managing resources, and engaging in self-development. Furthermore, interview participants noted that many of these master sergeant leadership duties have increased in importance or scope over the years.

Master Sergeant Leadership KSAOs

The next question we addressed was which leadership KSAOs are needed to perform master sergeant job duties well. In other words, what should be measured as part of the promotion system that will be a good predictor of leadership and performance as a master sergeant in the Air Force? In answering this question, we reviewed academic research on KSAOs related to leader effectiveness and collected information from our interviews with subject matter experts.

Research on Leadership KSAOs

Over the last several decades, researchers have developed and tested various theories of leadership effectiveness, including examining specific attributes or traits associated with effective leadership.[2] Therefore, as an initial source of information, we reviewed prior research on leadership KSAOs that may be important to consider when evaluating leadership potential as a master sergeant. Our review focused primarily on recent quantitative summaries that integrated results across many individual studies (i.e., meta-analysis) as well as more qualitative summaries of key attributes found to be predictive of leader effectiveness.[3] These previous studies highlight key knowledge and skills important for leadership as well as other characteristics, such as cognitive ability, personality, and past experiences that can influence leader performance through their impact on attainment of particular leadership knowledge and skills.

First, there has been some research examining leadership KSAOs in a military-specific context. For example, in an analysis of alternative predictors for U.S. Air Force junior officer selection and assessment, Ingerick, Schwartz, and Weismuller (2006) identified more than 50 aptitudes/abilities, cross-functional skills, and personal qualities underlying the Air Force leadership competencies (i.e., personal, people/ team, and institutional) described previously (see Table 2.4). Although they were identifying attributes for junior officer selection, the Air Force designates these same leadership competencies as applying to enlisted leadership levels as well.

---

[2] For reviews, see Avolio et al. (2003) and Bass and Bass (2008).

[3] For published reviews of research on leader attributes see Hoffman et al. (2011), Yukl (2006), Zaccaro (2007), and Zaccaro, Kemp, and Bader (2004).

Table 2.4. Attributes Underlying Air Force Leadership Competencies

Category	Attributes		Air Force Competencies
Aptitudes and abilities	• Abstract-analytical reasoning • Creative-divergent thinking • Critical thinking • Cognitive-integrative complexity • General mental ability	• Information processing and analysis • Moral reasoning • Practical intelligence • Problem-solving • Social-emotional intelligence • Systems thinking and planning	• Leading the institution • Leading people/teams • Personal leadership (exercise sound judgment; inspire trust; foster effective communication)
Cross-functional skills	• Basic computer skills • Conflict management and resolution skills • Decisionmaking skills • Dynamic information processing and analysis skills • Metacognitive and motivational skills • Negotiation skills • Persuasion skills • Problem-solving skills • Self-directed learning and development skills	• Self-management skills • Situational awareness skills • Social-interpersonal skills • Tacit knowledge • Teamwork skills • Verbal-written communication skills	• Leading the institution • Leading people/teams • Personal leadership (exercise sound judgment; adapt and perform under pressure; inspire trust; assess self; foster effective communication)
Personal qualities	• Achievement motivation • Adaptability • Affiliation motivation • Agreeableness • Conscientiousness • Creativity • Cultural tolerance • Dependability • Decisiveness • Dominance-surgency • Energy level-potency • Extraversion • Emotional maturity-stability • General self-esteem • Generalized self-efficacy • Initiative-proactive personality • Intellectance	• Integrity • (Internal) locus of control • Motivation to lead-socialized power motive • Motivation to learn • Openness to experience • Persistence/self-reliance • Risk propensity • Self-discipline • Self-monitoring/social perceptiveness • Service orientation • Sociability • Stress tolerance • Team orientation • Tolerance for ambiguity	• Leading the institution • Leading people/teams • Personal leadership (exercise sound judgment; adapt and perform under pressure; inspire trust; lead courageously; assess self)

SOURCE: Ingerick, Schwartz, and Weismuller, 2006.

There have also been a number of studies examining Army leadership KSAOs (e.g., Mumford, Yarkin-Levin, et al., 1986; Wisecarver et al., 2011). One study in particular conducted an extensive examination of current and future KSAOs important to consider in making promotion decisions across Army NCO pay grades (Ford et al., 2000). As part of the study, panels of subject matter experts ranked the top ten KSAOs predicted to be important for current and future Army NCO job requirements. For midlevel NCOs (E-6 and E-7), the panels identified the following ten KSAOs as important for job requirements in the 2000 to 2010 era:

- motivating and leading others
- Military Occupational Specialty-specific knowledge and skill
- judgment and decisionmaking
- common task knowledge and skill
- directing, monitoring, and supervising work
- characteristic level of integrity and discipline
- training others
- general cognitive aptitude
- oral communication skill
- physical fitness.

Additional KSAOs identified for SNCOs (E-8 and E-9) included:

- concern for soldier quality of life
- writing skills
- general self-management skill
- advanced computer skills.

Although this study was conducted in 2000, many of the KSAOs are consistent with the attributes identified as underlying the Air Force leadership competencies.

In addition to these military specific studies, there has been a considerable amount of research in academia on the KSAOs needed for effective leadership. Overall, research seems to have focused less on specific knowledge important for leadership, likely given the importance of the job context in determining key knowledge areas. However, researchers have identified the overall importance of general technical knowledge for effective leadership, which includes "knowledge about the methods, processes, and equipment for conducting the specialized activities of the managers' organizational unit" (Yukl, 2006, p. 192).

A considerably greater amount of research has examined specific skills and abilities needed for effective leadership. For example, a number of studies have examined the importance of general cognitive ability or intelligence, with overall findings from these studies indicating a moderate relationship between general cognitive ability and overall leader effectiveness (Judge, Colbert, and Ilies, 2004). Research has also found a relationship between more specific cognitive abilities, such as verbal reasoning and creative or divergent thinking, and leader achievement (Connelly et al., 2000).

Researchers have also identified a number of skills considered to be important for leader effectiveness, with recent work organizing previous conceptualizations of leadership skill requirements into the following four general categories (Mumford, Campion, and Morgeson, 2007):

- cognitive skills
- interpersonal skills
- business skills
- strategic skills.

Cognitive skills are defined as the underlying or foundational skill requirements and include skills related to speaking, active listening, writing, reading comprehension, and critical thinking. *Interpersonal skills* are defined as those skills that involve interacting with others and include skills related to social perceptiveness, coordination, negotiation, and persuasion. *Business skills* are defined as the skills related to a specific functional area and include skills related to operations analysis, management of personnel resources, management of financial resources, and management of materiel resources (e.g., equipment, facilities). *Strategic skills* are defined as the highly conceptual skills needed to take more of a systems perspective, and include skills related to visioning, systems perception and evaluation, identification of downstream consequences and key causes, problem identification, and solution appraisal. Overall, these skill categories also appear to do a good job at capturing the skills identified in the Air Force and Army specific studies described previously.

In addition to the knowledge, skills, and abilities listed above, researchers have identified other characteristics, such as personality attributes that are predictive of leader effectiveness. Personality can be defined as a person's typical patterns of behavior. These patterns of behavior, observed by others, form a person's reputation (Hogan, Hogan, and Roberts, 1996). This reputation, in terms of personality dimensions, can be reliably summarized into five broad dimensions known widely as the Big Five (Goldberg, 1993). These dimensions, which can be traced back to early work in the Air Force (Tupes and Christal, 1961), include the following (Goldberg, 1990):

- openness to experience (e.g., intellectual, curious, creative)
- conscientiousness (e.g., orderly, dependable, careful)
- extraversion (e.g., expressive, talkative, energetic)
- agreeableness (e.g., cooperative, considerate, affectionate)
- emotional stability (e.g., secure, calm, low anxiety).

Overall, research has shown that these Big Five dimensions are related to a variety of important outcomes, including task performance, contextual performance (e.g., helping others), and leadership (Barrick and Mount, 1991; Bono and Judge, 2004; Chiaburu et al., 2011; Judge, Bono, et al., 2002). For example, in a recent meta-analysis, researchers found strong support for the Big Five dimensions predicting leadership, with the dimensions of extraversion, openness to experience, and conscientiousness having the strongest relationship to leadership (Judge, Bono, et al., 2002).

Research has also found support for a relationship between leader effectiveness and other attributes beyond the Big Five. For example, in another meta-analysis, researchers found that characteristics such as achievement motivation, energy, and honesty/integrity were moderately related to leader effectiveness (Hoffman et al., 2011). A considerable amount of leadership research has also found support for the importance of general *charisma* on leader effectiveness (Judge and Piccolo, 2004). Finally, another research study found that *motivation to lead* predicted behavioral measures of leadership potential above and beyond other predictors such as general cognitive ability, values, personality, and attitudes (Chan and Drasgow, 2001).

Thus, previous military-specific and academic research on KSAOs required for effective leadership highlight a number of key attributes that are also likely important for leadership as a master sergeant in the Air Force.

Interview Findings

To gather more detailed information on the specific leadership KSAOs that might be important for master sergeants, we asked our interview participants to describe the KSAOs needed to perform the master sergeant duties they identified. Specific KSAOs and the percentage of interview participants who mentioned each are provided in Tables 2.5 to 2.7. Again, it is important to note that these proportions represent responses to open-ended questions. Therefore, the proportions should not be interpreted as the relative importance of each KSAO since interview participants generally relied upon memory to respond to these open-ended questions.

Knowledge Areas

As shown in Table 2.5, our interview participants identified a number of knowledge areas they viewed as important for master sergeants to fulfill their duties.

Table 2.5. Master Sergeant Leadership Knowledge Areas

Knowledge Areas	Percentage of Participants Identifying
One's technical area	87
Larger Air Force mission	59
Manpower and assignments	23
Budgetary systems	21
Air Force standards (i.e., rules and regulations) and core values	18
Training requirements	10
Other AFSCs	10

NOTE: *N* = 41. We only include attributes identified by at least 10 percent of participants.

15

In particular, the vast majority of interview participants (87 percent) indicated that knowledge of one's technical area (i.e., expertise related to one's AFSC) is critical for master sergeants to fulfill their technical task work, but also to provide good supervision and feedback. Additional knowledge areas, such as knowledge of manpower and assignments and budgetary systems, were identified as necessary to effectively manage resources. Finally, more-encompassing knowledge areas—such as knowledge of the larger Air Force mission, standards, and core values, as well as knowledge of training requirements and other AFSCs—were also identified as important to be a good leader as a master sergeant.

Skills and Abilities

As shown in Table 2.6, our interview participants identified a number of key skills they viewed as important in enabling master sergeants to fulfill their duties.

Table 2.6. Master Sergeant Leadership Skills and Abilities

Skills and Abilities	Percentage of Participants Identifying
Communication skills (verbal and written)	64
Human relations/Interpersonal skills	64
Problem solving skills	38
Strategic thinking skills	21
Organizational skills	15
Time management skills	13

NOTE: N = 41. We only include attributes identified by at least 10 percent of participants.

Consistent with the previously described research on general leadership skill categories (Mumford, Campion, and Morgeson, 2007), these include interpersonal skills, key cognitive skills (e.g., verbal and written communication), and important strategic skills, such as strategic thinking and problem solving. Organizational and time management skills could also fall under the category of "business skills" needed to effectively manage resources.

Other Characteristics

As shown in Table 2.7, our interview participants also identified a number of other personal attributes they viewed as important for master sergeants to possess so that they can fulfill their duties.

Table 2.7. Master Sergeant Leadership Knowledge, Skills, Abilities, and Other Characteristics

Other Characteristics	Percentage of Participants Identifying
Ambition/Initiative	56
Advanced degree (e.g., BA, BS, MA)	56
Selflessness	31
Loyalty	28
Inspirational	26
Physical fitness	26
Integrity	15
Experience across bases/positions	15
Maturity	10
Resolve/persistence	10

NOTE: N = 41. We only include KSAOs identified by at least 10 percent of participants.

Similar to some of the characteristics identified in prior leadership research, these other characteristics include attributes such as being selfless, inspirational, and having integrity and persistence. Participants also mentioned the importance of master sergeants having ambition and taking initiative in leadership situations, which is consistent with research on the importance of motivation to lead (Chan and Drasgow, 2001). Finally, participants said master sergeants ought to be physically fit and to have pursued higher education, making them good role models for other airmen.

Again, it is important to note that these proportions represent responses to open-ended questions, and the proportions should not be interpreted as the relative importance of KSAOs because interview participants generally relied upon memory to respond to these questions. However, many of the KSAOs identified by our subject matter experts are consistent with important leader KSAOs found in other research. Thus, although not completely comprehensive in nature, our review of the academic literature coupled with our interviews highlight several key areas of KSAOs important for effective performance as a master sergeant in the Air Force and provide a basis to assess the extent to which the current promotion system is effective at selecting those airmen who will have the KSAOs required of a master sergeant.

Summary

Master sergeants represent the first level of senior enlisted leadership in the Air Force and are expected to transition from being technical experts to leaders. Consistent with this Air Force expectation, our interview participants identified technical task work as a key duty, but further highlighted the increased importance of leadership duties at the master sergeant rank.

Furthermore, interview participants noted that many of these master sergeant leadership duties have increased in importance or scope over the years.

Findings from our interviews and our review of prior leadership studies then highlighted a number of different categories of KSAOs that master sergeants may require to be good leaders and to be able to perform their duties effectively. For example, both our interviews and prior research identified the importance of key technical knowledge. Similarly, four general categories of skills (i.e., cognitive skills, interpersonal skills, business/management skills, and strategic skills) seem to be consistently identified as important for leader effectiveness. In addition, prior research studies, as well as our interview participants, identified other characteristics—such as general cognitive ability, personality attributes, and motivation to lead—as important for leader effectiveness. Finally, interview participants highlighted the importance to the Air Force of having leaders who are physically fit and have pursued higher education, as these individuals tend to be good role models for airmen.

Thus, as master sergeants transition from technical experts to leaders of operational competence with increased leadership responsibilities, those KSAOs identified as necessary to performing these increased leadership duties will be important to measure as part of the promotion system. Furthermore, many of these attributes, such as cognitive ability, personality, and motivation to lead are less malleable. Therefore, deficiencies cannot be addressed through simple training.

3. The Weighted Airman Promotion System

WAPS, the tool used by the Air Force to select enlisted airmen for promotion, was formally instituted in 1970. Prior to that, the Air Force used a decentralized board process in which promotion allocations were distributed to MAJCOMs based on Air Force–wide vacancies within each AFSC.[1] MAJCOMs then delegated promotion allocations to subordinate unit commanders, who conducted their own review boards to select the best candidates. Over time, airmen began to perceive inequities in the promotion allocations across AFSCs and voiced strong objections to the decentralized promotion system, which lacked standardization in the board procedures used by different commanders (Hall and Nelsen, 1980).

This discontent led to a congressional investigation that found that the decentralized board process posed unnecessary limitations on individuals and recommended that significant changes be made to the promotion process.[2] At the same time the congressional investigation was taking place, the Air Force Human Resources Laboratory (AFHRL) was in the process of developing WAPS to address these concerns. WAPS was intended to offer a less subjective approach compared to its historical predecessor and was designed to help leaders determine which airmen are best qualified for promotion to the next grade through objective scores and weighted factors.[3] Since its inception, there have been minor changes to testing standards, content, and weights, but the main features of the promotion system remain largely unchanged, even despite prior reviews and recommendations.

In this chapter, we describe the Air Force's current promotion system and implementation of WAPS.[4]

Promotion Eligibility

Although there are a number of different factors that can disqualify an airmen from being promotion eligible (see U.S. Air Force, 2009c), the main eligibility requirements for promotion are meeting minimum requirements for the amount of time served in the current grade (TIG) and the amount of time served on active duty or total amount of time in service (TIS). For promotion to E-5 through E-7, airmen must also meet a minimum skill level. Skill levels signify that an airman has reached an increased level of job knowledge and proficiency. They are awarded when

---

[1] AFSCs represent different enlisted jobs in the Air Force, with each AFSC represented by a numerical code identifying the specific career group, field, functional area, and skill level.

[2] See *Improvements in Enlisted Promotion Policy*, U.S. Congress Report, p. 11074, as cited in Hall and Nelsen, 1980, p. 50.

[3] See Horace Wade, address to special Subcommittee on Enlisted Promotion Policy, Committee on Armed Services, House of Representatives, August 22, 1967, as cited in cited in Hall and Nelsen, 1980, p. 47.

[4] See U.S. Air Force (2009c) for full details on the enlisted promotion system.

an airman is certified in the tasks identified in his/her on-the-job training records and successfully passes tests appropriate to that skill level. Table 3.1 identifies the TIG, TIS, and skill-level eligibility requirements for promotion to each grade.

Table 3.1. Main Promotion Eligibility Criteria for Each Eligible Promotion Grade

Eligible Promotion Grade	TIG	TIS	Skill Level
Airman (E-2)	6 months	n/a	n/a
Airman First Class (E-3)	10 months[a]	n/a	n/a
Senior Airman (E-4)	20 months	3 years[b]	n/a
Staff Sergeant (E-5)	6 months	3 years	5 level
Technical Sergeant (E-6)	23 months	5 years	7 level
Master Sergeant (E-7)	24 months	8 years	7 level
Senior Master Sergeant (E-8)	20 months	11 years	n/a
Chief Master Sergeant (E-9)	21 months	14 years	n/a

[a] According to U.S. Air Force (2009c), "individuals initially enlisting for a period of 6 years are promoted from Airman to Airman First Class upon completion of either technical training or 20 weeks of technical training (start date of the 20 week period is the date of Basic Military Training (BMT) completion), whichever occurs first."
[b] Airmen are also eligible if they reach 28 months TIG, whichever occurs first.

Airmen selected for promotion to staff sergeant, master sergeant, and senior master sergeant must also complete specific in-residence PME requirements before assuming the grade. Staff sergeants must complete Airman Leadership School (ALS); master sergeants must complete Noncommissioned Officer Academy (NCOA); and senior master sergeant must complete Senior Noncommissioned Officer Academy (SNCOA).

The number of eligible airmen promoted annually to each higher grade is determined by a quota system. The quotas are set by Headquarters United States Air Force (HQ USAF) based on a combination of fiscal and statutory constraints and projected vacancies for each grade (U.S. Air Force, 2009b, p. 6). Consequently, changes to the Department of Defense budget and fluctuations in retention rates ensure that the quotas change every year for each grade. To ensure fairness, the quotas for each grade are applied evenly across every AFSC, so that an equal percentage of airmen are promoted within every AFSC (rates may vary slightly, depending upon rounding within an AFSC), with the following exceptions:

Chronic Critical Shortage (CCS) and Donor AFSCs: Based on shortages in manpower in certain AFSCs, the Air Force identifies a number of select AFSCs as having a CCS. These CCS AFSCs are promoted at a higher rate than the rest of the specialties (U.S. Air Force, 2009b, p. 19). To offset the higher selection rate for AFSCs designated as CCS, the Air Force also designates certain AFSCs as "donor" AFSCs, which have promotion rates below the standard promotion rate.

USAF Band and USAF Academy Band membership: Due to the specialized nature of band positions and a limited amount of personnel, promotions are granted solely based on existing vacancies. Therefore, USAF Band and USAF Academy band members are promoted separately from the rest of the force (U.S. Air Force, 2009b, p. 48).

Promotion Factors

There are several factors that determine who is selected for promotion, and they vary by grade. Airmen in grades E-1 to E-3 are promoted to the next grade automatically once they meet the minimum TIG and TIS requirements noted in Table 3.1 and assuming they do not have any adverse performance or disciplinary reports.[5] Promotions to E-5 through E-9 are based on a composite score of airmen's earned points on several different factors. The composite score is based on a compensatory model in which individuals who do not score well on one factor can compensate with more points on other factors. The factors and total number of points possible vary for promotions to E-5 through E-7 and promotions to E-8 and E-9. Table 3.2 outlines the factors and total possible points for each eligible promotion grade. Next, we provide more details on each WAPS factor.

Table 3.2. Total Possible Points for WAPS Factors

WAPS Factor	Total Possible Points for Promotion to E-5 through E-7	Total Possible Points for Promotion to E-8 and E-9
Specialty knowledge test (SKT)	100	NA
Promotion Fitness Exam (PFE)	100	NA
USAF Supervisory Exam (USAFSE)	NA	100
TIS	40	25
TIG	60	60
Decorations	25	25
EPR	135	135
Board Score	-	450
Maximum Possible Points	460	795

NOTE: NA = Not applicable.

Knowledge Tests

There are three different knowledge tests used as part of WAPS. For promotion to E-5 through E-7, candidates have to take the SKT and PFE. For promotion to E-8 and E-9, candidates take the USAFSE.

---

[5] For further details, see U.S. Air Force (2009b).

21

Specialty Knowledge Test

The SKT is a 100-question, multiple-choice test that measures important technical knowledge for each AFSC, with points for WAPS based on the percentage of questions answered correctly. Questions are developed annually by SNCOs within each career field using material from a variety of sources, such as the Career Field Education and Training Plan and occupational data. There is a separate SKT developed for each AFSC and each grade.[6] In certain AFSCs, such as a special-duty AFSC, and for airmen who have recently cross-trained into a new AFSC, there is no associated SKT. For these airmen, their PFE score is counted twice.

Promotion Fitness Exam

The PFE is a 100-question, multiple-choice test that measures general Air Force and supervisory knowledge, with points for WAPS based on the percentage of questions answered correctly. Material for the test is taken from Air Force Pamphlet 36-2241, *Professional Development Guide* (U.S. Air Force, 2009b), and spans a broad range of military knowledge, including history, organization, regulations, practices, traditions, and customs. For testing security purposes, two versions of the PFE are developed for each eligible promotion grade every year.

U.S. Air Force Supervisory Exam

This USAFSE is only applicable for E-8 and E-9 promotions and is the only knowledge test used for promotion to these grades. The USAFSE is a 100-question, multiple-choice test that ". . . evaluates practical military, supervisory, and managerial knowledge required in the top two NCO grades." Like the PFE, the material is taken from the Professional Development Guide. For test security purposes, two versions are developed for each eligible promotion grade every year. Points for WAPS are again based on the percent of questions correct on the test.

Time in Service and Time in Grade

To reflect the importance of experience, airmen also receive points for TIS and TIG as part of WAPS. As described previously, TIS is the amount of total time served on active duty in the Air Force. For purposes of promotion, TIS is computed as of the first day of the last months of the promotion cycle, including the first month if the individual served at least 15 days inclusive. For promotions to E-5 through E-7, airmen can earn two points for each year of TIS up to 20 years and one-sixth point for each month. Those airmen eligible for promotion to E-8 or E-9 receive one-twelfth point for each month of TIS, up to 25 years.

TIG is the amount of total time served in the individual's current pay grade (i.e., rank). Like TIS, TIG is computed as of the first day of the last month of the promotion cycle. The TIG total is scored by adding a half-point for each month in the current grade, up to 10 years.

---

[6] The one exception to this is that the same test is used for airmen eligible for promotion to the grades of E-6 and E-7.

Performance

The Air Force currently measures performance using two factors in WAPS, a decorations score and the EPR score.

Decorations

Enlisted airmen can earn up to 25 WAPS points for certain medals they are awarded.[7] Each medal is worth a different number of points based on the selectivity for each award (see U.S. Air Force, 2009b).

Enlisted Performance Report

The EPR is intended as the primary measure of duty performance and potential and is completed once per year by the immediate supervisor or anytime supervisors change (if they have at least 120 days of supervision) (U.S. Air Force, 2009b, p. 6). There are two EPR forms, one for airman basic through technical sergeant (E-1 to E-6),[8] and one for master sergeant through chief master sergeant (E-7 to E-9). Examples of each EPR form can be found in Appendix A. Each form is composed of several different sections. The first page of the EPR contains personal identification information, a job description, and a section for key duties, tasks and responsibilities. The remainder of the front side contains several sections for the "Rater" (i.e., the immediate supervisor) to assess performance. These sections require the supervisor to rate the airman's performance in several different areas on a four-point scale (from "Does Not Meet" to "Clearly Exceeds"). For airman in pay grades E-1 to E-6, performance is rated in the following areas: (1) primary/additional duties, (2) standards, conduct, character, and military bearing, (3) fitness, (4) training requirements, and (5) teamwork/followership. For airmen in paygrades E-7 to E-9, performance is rated in the following areas: (1) primary duties, (2) standards: enforcement and personal adherence, conduct, character, military bearing and customs and courtesies, (3) fitness, (4) resource management and decision making, (5) training, education, off-duty education, PME, professional enhancement and communication, and (6) leadership/team building/followership/mentorship. Supervisors also have space within each section to write several lines of information to summarize performance during the rating period.

The back side of the EPR provides an overall performance rating of 1 through 5 from both the Rater and the "Additional Rater" (the next supervisor up the chain). This overall performance rating is what is used in the WAPS calculation for the EPR factor for all grades. Airmen receive points for EPRs within the last five years, not to exceed ten reports. A weighted factor, which

---

[7] Medals include the Medal of Honor, AF/Navy/Distinguished Service Crosses, Defense Distinguished Service Medal, Distinguished Service Medal, Silver Star, Legion of Merit, Defense Superior Service Medal, Distinguished Flying Cross, Airman's/Soldier's/Navy-Marine Corps/Coast Guard/Bronze Star/Defense Meritorious Service Medals, Purple Heart, Air/Aerial Achievement/AF/Army/Navy/Joint Services/Coast Guard Commendation Medals, and AF/Navy/Army/Coast Guard/Joint Service Achievement Medals.

[8] According to U.S. Air Force (2009b), personnel in the grades of E-1 to E-3 with less than 20 months of TIS do not receive EPRs.

decreases as reports get older, is applied to each EPR for a maximum of 135 points added to the WAPS composite score.[9]

Board Score

Selection for the two highest pay grades of E-8 and E-9 also includes a board score based on the ratings of a three-member panel. Panels are organized by functional area and consist of one colonel and two chief master sergeants; the chief master sergeants are selected from the two largest career fields being reviewed by each individual panel.[10] The panel reviews the following documents for each eligible airman:

- all EPRs for the past ten years
- citations for all decorations
- Senior NCO Evaluation Brief (a computer-generated snapshot of the airman's career)
- Article 15/Nonjudicial Punishment (If applicable and determined to be filed by appropriate commander)
- record of courts-martial
- Air Force Form 77 (Letter of Evaluation when a full completed EPR was not available due to breaks in service, EPR appeals, administrative correction, etc.).

Overall, the panel members are intended to consider performance, leadership, breadth of experience, job responsibility, professional competence, specific achievements, and education in developing a final rating. Each panel member independently reviews and scores every record in the panel, with scores ranging from six to ten points in half-point increments. If two panel members' scores on a record differ by1.5 points or more, a "split" has occurred and must be resolved before calculating a final score. To resolve the split, all panel members discuss the record. Only those members involved in the split can change their scores, however. The split is considered resolved when at least one member agrees to change his/her score so that the difference is less than 1.5 points. Once all splits are resolved, the three panel scores for each record are totaled and multiplied by a factor of 15 to provide a final board score, which ranges from 270 to 450 points.

---

[9] For a more detailed explanation of the EPR scoring process, see U.S. Air Force (2009b).

[10] Although panel members won't be representative of all the career fields under their review, they are representative of the functional area of those career fields (e.g., there are medical panels, maintenance panels, support panels, etc.). The colonel will be a sitting or graduated group commander in the functional area, and the chief master sergeants will represent the two largest AFSCs within that functional area. Thus, although some AFSCs with very small numbers may not have direct representation on a panel, their records will still be viewed by someone within their functional area. The goal of this structure is to ensure that similar AFSCs are grouped together, while still trying to spread the workload across the panels in a manageable way.

Promotion Selection

Individual WAPS factor scores are totaled to produce a composite score for every airman eligible for promotion. Based on the Air Force established quotas for vacancies in each grade, a cutoff score is derived for each AFSC. It is important to note that eligible airmen compete for promotion only within their AFSC. Airmen whose composite score is above the cutoff for their AFSC are selected for promotion.[11] In cases where multiple individuals have the same score at the cutoff point, the Air Force promotes everyone with that score.

Summary

To correct perceived inequalities in the previous enlisted promotion system, WAPS was developed to provide a more transparent, objective, and fair system for selecting airmen to be promoted to the next higher grade. The system includes weighted factors intended to measure key knowledge, experience, and performance that allow airmen to more easily assess their probability of promotion.

Although master sergeants are the first tier of senior enlisted leadership, they are currently selected using the same promotion factors and weights as for promotion to E-5 and E-6. Consistent with the expectation that they are transitioning from being technical experts to leaders, the SKT, which measures technical knowledge, is a factor in their WAPS score. However, other factors intended to measure leadership potential for promotion to E-8 and E-9, such as a board score, are not included for promotion to master sergeant.

---

[11] Although the majority of airmen get promoted through WAPS, there are a few other avenues for promotion in specialized cases. For example, the Air Force has two programs, Senior Airmen Below-the-Zone and Stripes for Exceptional Performers, in which a select number of airmen can get promoted based on merit. The Air Force also has special promotion consideration for Prisoners of War/Missing in Action, declared national emergency or war, Congressional Medal of Honor recipients, prior service airmen, Wounded Warriors, and posthumous promotions. Finally, the Chief of Staff of the Air Force is also authorized to promote any enlisted airman to the next higher rank.

4. Effectiveness of the Current Master Sergeant Promotion System

In this chapter, we examine the extent to which WAPS is effective at promoting airmen who will be able to fulfill the leadership responsibilities of a master sergeant in the Air Force. It is important to note that we are not able to empirically determine if WAPS is actually selecting the right airmen to be promoted to master sergeant, given that we do not have data on how well those individuals not selected for promotion to master sergeant might have performed. However, we can examine the extent to which WAPS is assessing key leadership KSAOs required to perform well as a master sergeant (see Chapter Two).

In general, scholars have broadly described job performance as a function of three components: declarative knowledge, procedural knowledge and skill, and motivation. Declarative knowledge is "the knowledge of facts, rules, principles;" whereas procedural knowledge and skills reflect "the capability attained when . . . (knowing what to do) has been successfully combined with knowing how and being able to perform a task," (McCloy, Campbell, and Cudeck, 1994, p. 494). Following this distinction, it can be shown that declarative knowledge is necessary but not sufficient for successful job performance. For example, an individual may know the basic mechanics for flying a fighter jet (declarative knowledge) but may not have developed the skills to safely perform simple aerial maneuvers (procedural knowledge and skill). The third component influencing performance is motivation, which reflects an individual's decision to exert some amount of effort toward an objective. Although some tasks may be completed with minimal levels of motivation (e.g., answering a phone call), succeeding at more complex tasks often requires greater levels of persistence and motivation. Ideally, all three of these performance determinants should be assessed to identify the most effective candidate for promotion. Additionally, scholars have proposed and found some support for other characteristics, such as cognitive ability, personality, and past experiences influencing leader performance through their impact on attainment of particular leadership knowledge and skills (Connelly et al., 2000; Mumford, Zaccaro, et al., 2000; Van Iddekinge, Ferris, and Heffner, 2009; Zaccaro et al., 2004). Thus, these more indirect determinants can also provide useful measures of leadership potential.

We first examine the extent to which the current WAPS factors provide good assessments of key master sergeant leadership KSAOs described in Chapter Two, including the extent to which declarative knowledge, procedural knowledge and skills, and motivation are all assessed as part of the promotion system. We then present findings from our interviews regarding perceptions of the overall effectiveness of the current promotion system. Finally, we examine how WAPS is functioning in terms of the relative influence of each factor on current promotion outcomes.

Knowledge, Skills, and Abilities Assessed by WAPS

As described in Chapter Three, WAPS uses a compensatory model composed of six weighted factors to determine promotion outcomes to master sergeant:

- SKT
- PFE
- TIS
- TIG
- Decorations
- EPR.

As we will describe in the following sections, these combined factors appear to be important direct and indirect (or proxy) measures of key declarative knowledge, procedural knowledge and skills, and other characteristics, such as motivation to lead as identified in Chapter Two.

Job Knowledge Tests: SKT and PFE

Findings from our interviews with subject matter experts and review of prior research indicated that knowledge of one's technical area (i.e., technical expertise) as well as general Air Force knowledge related to the mission and management of resources, such as manpower, budgets, and training, are important to perform well as a master sergeant in the Air Force. Currently, both the SKT and PFE are designed to directly measure such declarative knowledge. The SKT is designed to measure important technical knowledge for each Air Force Specialty, and the PFE is designed to measure a broad range of military and leadership knowledge.[1] The extent to which the PFE measures the key leadership knowledge most important for a master sergeant should be further examined, however.

Furthermore, research on job knowledge tests used in other contexts has found them to be excellent predictors of overall performance (Dye, Reck, and McDaniel, 1993; Schmidt and Hunter, 1998) as well as leadership knowledge (Connelly et al., 2000). In fact, job knowledge tests are among one of the best predictors of general performance (Schmidt and Hunter, 1998),[2] and causal models demonstrate that job knowledge makes a strong contribution to task proficiency (Borman, Pulakos, et al., 1991). Job knowledge tests have also been found to be predictive of both typical as well as peak levels of performance (Ones and Viswesvaran, 2007). That is, individuals who score well on a job knowledge test are more likely to perform well in day-to-day job performance as well as performing well in situations that demand very high or maximum levels of performance.

---

[1] Note that it was not within the scope of this study to conduct an in-depth evaluation of how well the SKT and PFE are developed, such as the quality of test items. Our analysis is based on their potential as general knowledge tests and published information on their general content.

[2] The most recent meta-analysis examining the relationship between job knowledge tests and performance found them to have an estimated validity of 0.48 (Schmidt and Hunter, 1998).

Although job knowledge tests are designed to measure a candidate's ability to perform a job and are among the best predictors of performance, the tests primarily measure declarative knowledge rather than procedural knowledge and skills. For example, although the PFE is intended to measure important knowledge related to leadership, it does not necessarily assess the extent to which individuals would actually be able to apply that knowledge or the extent to which they may have successfully demonstrated those leadership skills in the past. Knowledge tests alone are also not able to capture other skills and attributes, such as personality traits, that may be important for performance. Therefore, additional measures can be used to supplement job knowledge tests to improve the overall prediction of job performance and increase the probability of promoting successful candidates. Nonetheless, these results suggest that job knowledge tests are a potentially valuable tool for identifying airmen for promotion.

Job Experience: TIS and TIG

The job experience factors of TIS and TIG may not be direct measures of specific KSAOs, but they are likely good indirect or proxy measures of declarative and procedural knowledge and skills that are likely predictive of performance as a master sergeant. Job experience is defined by the accumulation of job knowledge that is generally gained by fulfilling responsibilities associated with a specific job (Quiñones, Ford, and Teachout, 1995; Sturman, 2003). In general, research has shown that individuals with more experience have greater levels of job performance as well as more job knowledge (Schmidt, Outerbridge, et al., 1988).

However, research has shown that the relationship between experience and performance can differ based on the measure of experience as well as the complexity of the job. For example, a comprehensive meta-analysis (i.e., a quantitative summary that integrated results across many individual studies) found that job tenure has a slightly stronger relationship with job performance compared to organizational tenure (Quiñones et al., 1995). However, the meta-analysis did not differentiate between studies examining the relationship between job tenure and job performance in current and future jobs; therefore, the findings may reflect individuals' performance in their current jobs rather than predicting their performance in a different job. This is an important distinction, because the Air Force uses TIG to select airmen for promotion to a higher-ranking job. Consequently, the relationship between TIG and performance may be lower to the extent that the future job has different responsibilities requiring different KSAOs.

Additionally, although previous research has shown that experience may be a stronger predictor of performance in less complex jobs (McDaniel, Schmidt, and Hunter, 1988), a more recent meta-analysis found that for complex jobs, the strength of the correlation between job experience and performance increases as the mean level of experience increases (Sturman, 2003). In other words, job experience would still be a moderate predictor of job performance for a sample of applicants who have more than eight years of experience. The results, however, were in the opposite direction when examining organizational tenure (analogous to TIS) rather than job experience. That is, organizational tenure was not a good predictor of job performance for individuals with more than several years of tenure with an organization. These findings suggest that job experience rather than seniority is a valid predictor for individuals with considerable experience and tenure within an organization.

As mentioned previously, the type of experience (e.g., supervisory) in addition to the amount of experience can be measured. In a study of early career managers, experience in a managerial role but not tenure with the organization was an important predictor of objective performance (e.g., sales) (McEnrue, 1988). Similarly, a recent study on Army NCOs found that leadership experiences were related to an NCO's knowledge, skills, and abilities, which ultimately related to leader performance (Van Iddenkinge et al., 2009). A separate study of Army NCOs also found that early supervisory experience had a direct effect on supervisors' proficiency, as measured in an assessment center by performance on tasks typically performed by supervisors (Borman, Hanson, et al., 1993). Additionally, it was found that the Army NCOs' abilities were directly related to the amount of their supervisory experience. The researchers interpreted this finding as an indication that those NCOs with high ability were provided with greater opportunities for supervisory responsibility. Therefore, it's possible that technical sergeants in the Air Force who have considerable supervisory experience may be better able and prepared to take on a supervisory role.

Taken together, research on job experience suggests that relevant role experience (e.g., supervisory experiences) would be a good predictor of job performance. Further, a measure of experience is likely to complement other WAPS components (such as the knowledge tests) by measuring the extent to which airmen have been able to apply and practice relevant knowledge and skills. However, given that organizational tenure tends to be a weaker predictor of performance as individuals' tenure increases beyond several years, in the Air Force context, it is expected that TIG may be a stronger predictor of master sergeant job performance compared to TIS.

Past Performance: EPR and Decorations

The Air Force currently attempts to assess past performance using two factors in WAPS, the EPR rating and a decorations score. The current performance dimensions on the EPR for NCO ranks include (1) primary/additional duties, (2) standards, conduct, character, and military bearing, (3) fitness, (4) training requirements, and (5) teamwork/followership (including leadership if appropriate for the rank). The rater is then intended to consider these dimensions when providing an overall performance rating that is ultimately included in WAPS.[3] Therefore, if accurate ratings are provided, the extent to which airmen perform well in these categories should provide a measure of related procedural knowledge and skills as well as motivation. Certainly, the EPR could be revised to measure performance dimensions related to other key

---

[3] For a more detailed explanation of the EPR rating process, see U.S. Air Force (2011).

skills and abilities identified in Chapter Two. Similarly, as a reflection of prior successful performance, decorations may indirectly measure important KSAOs.

Overall, these measures have the potential to be effective factors in a promotion system, as past performance is generally regarded as one of the best predictors of future performance. For example, in a study examining variables related to supervisor ratings of Army soldier performance, researchers found that past performance ratings of soldier dependability and technical proficiency were related to supervisory performance ratings (Borman, White, et al., 1995). Similarly, in one of the largest validation studies conducted for the Army (Project A),[4] researchers found not only that past performance was a good predictor of future performance, but also that past performance in technical jobs was a good predictor of future leadership and supervisory performance (Oppler, McCloy, and Campbell, 2001). These results further suggested that two components—ratings of leadership potential and effort—provided additional benefits to the prediction of future performance above and beyond traditional test measures (i.e., Armed Services Vocational Aptitude Battery). Based on their findings, the researchers concluded that there is strong evidence for using measures of job performance as a basis for promotion.

Predictive Validity Assessment

To provide further evidence for the effectiveness of these factors in selecting airmen for promotion to master sergeant, we attempted to examine the extent to which these WAPS factors are predictive of future job performance as a master sergeant in the Air Force, known as predictive validity.[5] We found that there is little variance in supervisor ratings of overall performance at the master sergeant rank though. Therefore, we did not have an ideal measure of master sergeant performance with which to examine predictive validity. In consideration of several alternatives, promotion board scores of master sergeants who are eligible for promotion to E-8 have sufficient variance and are believed to reflect the performance of a master sergeant. Therefore, we could examine the relationship between scores on the WAPS factors for technical sergeants selected for promotion to master sergeant and later board scores as a master sergeant

---

[4] Conducted in the 1980s and 1990s, the Army undertook a large-scale effort known as Project A to examine and improve the Army's personnel selection and classification systems. Tens of thousands of soldiers from a broad range of Army jobs were included in the research (see Campbell and Knapp, 2001).

[5] The most common way to assess predictive validity is to examine the correlation or degree of association between scores on the selection measure and the criterion of interest (e.g., performance). Correlations range from zero to one, with one indicating a perfect relationship and zero indicating no relationship between the selection measure and the criterion. Correlations can also be positive or negative. A positive correlation indicates that as scores on one variable increase, so do scores on the other variable. In contrast, a negative correlation indicates that as scores on one variable increase, scores on the other variable decrease. In the case of promotion, we generally expect to see positive correlations. For example, we would expect that people who score higher on the SKT as a technical sergeant would have higher performance ratings for their technical work as a master sergeant. The stronger the correlation between the two scores, the more useful it is for determining promotions. For further information, see Society for Industrial and Organizational Psychology, Inc. (SIOP) 2003.

eligible for promotion to E-8.[6] Board members review specific information related to many of the WAPS factors as part of their evaluation (i.e., TIS, TIG, decorations, EPR). Consequently, any observed relationship between the WAPS factors and the promotion board score may just reflect a board preference for certain characteristics instead of a true measure of actual performance. The two WAPS factors that are not included in the records reviewed by board members are the SKT and PFE. For these factors, correlations with promotion board scores ranged from 0.16 to 0.28 for the SKT and 0.16 to 0.29 for the PFE across AFSCs.[7] Although these estimates are not large in size, they do provide some evidence indicating that technical sergeants who score high on the SKT and PFE are more likely to be viewed as having performed well as a master sergeant.[8] It will be important for future research to try to obtain unbiased measures of job performance for research purposes to further establish the predictive validity of the promotion system.

Thus, the current WAPS factors have the potential to either directly or indirectly measure many of the key declarative knowledge, procedural knowledge and skills, motivation, and other characteristics important for performing well as a master sergeant in the Air Force. Specifically, the SKT and PFE are intended to provide direct measures of important declarative knowledge. TIS and TIG likely provide indirect or proxy measures of declarative and procedural knowledge and skills. The EPR and decorations scores are intended to provide direct and indirect measures of key procedural knowledge and skills and motivation through an assessment of past performance.

Interview Findings

To further explore the effectiveness of the promotion system, we asked interview participants about their perceptions of the effectiveness of the current promotion system in selecting master sergeants who would be good leaders and whether they saw gaps in the KSAOs of current master sergeants. Our findings from these interviews are described here.

---

[6] Once eligible for promotion to senior master sergeant, all master sergeants receive a board score that includes an assessment of performance as a master sergeant based on the board's review of records.

[7] All correlations were significant due to the large sample size.

[8] Using data from promotion cycles across the years 1996 through 2008, we examined the correlations between the WAPS scores of technical sergeants selected for promotion to master sergeant and their follow-on promotion board score once a master sergeant eligible for promotion to senior master sergeant (E-8). Given potential differences by AFSC and promotion cycle, we first calculated these correlations separately for each AFSC within a promotion cycle. We then created a weighted average across AFSCs for each promotion cycle. Total sample sizes ranged from 1,600 to 2,994 across promotion cycles, with 46 to 77 AFSCs having enough records to analyze per promotion cycle. The correlations reported in the text have been corrected for restriction of range. This correction estimates the correlations if everyone who appears in the dataset was selected for promotion to master sergeant and had at least one board score. This correction is important because those who fail to get promoted may be expected to do worse on average than those who are selected for promotion. See Sackett and Yang (2000) for more information on correcting for range restriction.

Gaps in KSAOs

Overall, participants in our interviews stated that the vast majority of current master sergeants are excellent airmen. However, participants indicated that in some cases, they believed technical sergeants who were not ready for the increased leadership responsibilities were being promoted to master sergeant. In particular, 31 percent of participants indicated that they see a lack of motivation to be a leader in some master sergeants. Related to this, some participants also identified a lack of maturity (26 percent of participants) and lack of a general level of engagement among some master sergeants (21 percent of participants). One respondent stated, "I think we have a lot of master sergeants that haven't really embraced the concept that they are not a technical expert—a lot of master sergeants still behave as if they are really just super technical sergeants." Similarly, another respondent stated, "I think we have a lot of master sergeants that don't transition well. They want to remain comfortable and want people to continue to tell them what to do and how to do it."

Some participants also expressed concern that not all master sergeants were meeting their PME requirements or engaging in further professional development, such as enrolling in higher education courses (18 percent of participants). According to the U.S. Air Force (2009a), master sergeants are expected to complete the Community College of the Air Force (CCAF) degree for their AFSC as well as immediately enroll in and complete the SNCOA upon selection for promotion to master sergeant. Furthermore, pursuing and completing PME requirements is outlined as part of SNCO responsibilities to "secure and promote PME and professional enhancement courses for themselves and subordinates to develop and cultivate leadership skills and military professionalism" (p. 13). However, data show that roughly 30 percent of master sergeants never complete SNCOA. Related to this, one of our interview respondents stated,

> Based on my experience, there is a correlation of master sergeants who don't do the PME and CCAF and a lower level of performance to their general and specific competencies. If they don't do the fundamental expectations levied upon their grade, I find that they don't perform at a higher level in other areas too, or they pick and choose which of the competencies to perform at a level commensurate with their grade. Master sergeants who do the PME and degree more often will perform all at a high level.

Finally, some participants also mentioned gaps in master sergeants' level of communication skills (18 percent of participants) and knowledge of the bigger Air Force mission (13 percent of participants). For example, one participant stated, "I do see a gap in not being able to understand the strategic picture. They are focusing on the six-feet targets, not six months out, and not seeing the sum total of their squads' contribution to the overall picture."

Some of these gaps can be addressed through training and education, such as improving communication skills. However, other gaps, such as a lack of motivation to lead, may be better addressed through the promotion process.

Perceptions of the Effectiveness of the Current Promotion Process to Master Sergeant

A majority of the participants we interviewed (77 percent) indicated that the current promotion system needs some improvement. As one respondent stated, "I don't think it is effective anymore because the transition from technical sergeant to master sergeant is one of the most significant transitions airmen will have in their career because the knowledge, skills, and expectations are so much greater between those two grades."

The biggest concern voiced by almost all of the participants we interviewed (91 percent) was that EPR scores were inflated, with almost all airmen receiving the highest overall performance rating possible. Because only this overall performance rating is included in WAPS, participants voiced further concerns that WAPS lacked a good measure of leadership potential (21 percent of participants), with promotions being driven only by knowledge test scores on the PFE and SKT (26 percent), and too much emphasis on TIS and TIG (also 26 percent). One respondent stated,

> Someone regardless of performance history and short of a referral EPR
> can make master sergeant because it is merely a mathematical
> computation. All the individual has to do is overcome shortcomings
> through a test.

Similarly, another respondent commented that the current system "says if you hang in there long enough, then you can get promoted, and I don't think that's how we want to pick our people."[9] In summary, one respondent stated,

> If we don't promote the right people, we lose our edge over the adversary
> . . . it is the people that make a difference. We have to select the right
> people for the right job.

Relative Influence of WAPS Factors

As summarized previously, our review of the current WAPS factors indicated that they have the potential to be important direct and indirect (or proxy) measures of key declarative knowledge, procedural knowledge and skills, and other characteristics, such as motivation to lead, identified in Chapter Two. Although each WAPS factor has an intended weight in the promotion system due to the range of available points, differences in the variance of scores on each factor (such as the concerns expressed by our interview participants) will affect the actual influence each factor has on promotion outcomes. Therefore, to examine how WAPS is currently functioning in terms of what factors have the greatest influence on promotion to master sergeant, we modeled promotion outcomes by AFSC using a statistical technique known as a generalized boosted model (GBM).

GBM is a flexible option for modeling dichotomous outcomes, such as promoted/not promoted, and calculates the "relative influence" of each explanatory variable on an outcome.

---

[9] See Appendix C for a summary of descriptive statistics on WAPS factor scores and the relationship between scores on factors for those individuals selected for promotion to master sergeant.

Out of all of the variation explained by the model, the relative influence is the percentage that is attributable to each explanatory variable. This measure is also insensitive to rescaling the explanatory variables, which makes it particularly appealing for this application. More details on GBM can be found in Appendix D.

For our analysis, we used data on the WAPS factor scores for all airmen eligible for promotion to master sergeant in 2000 to 2010 promotion cycles by AFSC. Although promotions occur on an annual basis, we collapsed the data across promotion cycles and limited our analysis to AFSCs that had at least 200 records. With too few observations, one or two variables might appear to contain all of the influence by chance alone. Further, the cross-validation process used to select the model uncertainty can be unreliable with too few observations.[10] This resulted in a total of 140 AFSCs in the analysis and a total sample size of 207,366.

Figure 4.1 shows the relative influence of each WAPS factor on promotion outcomes across AFSCs. As the figure shows, the relative influence of each factor varies widely across AFSCs. For example, the PFE accounts for close to 50 percent of promotion outcomes for some AFSCs, while it only accounts for around 20 percent in others. Overall, the PFE has a greater influence than the SKT for 63 percent of AFSCs and a greater influence than TIG for 95 percent. The SKT has a greater influence than TIG in 78 percent of AFSCs. The reason for such variation in influence on promotion outcomes is due to differences in the variance of scores on the WAPS factors by AFSC. In particular, we know that the knowledge tests, the PFE and SKT, are newly developed every year, with a specific SKT for each AFSC. As a result, the knowledge tests are likely to vary in difficulty from one year to the next, and across AFSCs. The long-term consequences that stem from this lack of standardization not only include variation in how well these tests are likely to predict future performance, but also variation in how much these test scores contribute to promotion decisions. This issue has been previously addressed in a study by Schiefer et al. (2008), which recommended standardizing scores for the SKT and PFE across AFSCs to ensure that test scores carry equal weight. Given this continued variance in the influence across AFSCs, the Air Force may wish to revisit whether test scores should be rescaled to ensure sufficient variance and similar weighting across AFSCs.

---

[10] We conducted the same analysis without collapsing data across years. However, we could only model the relative influence for a small number of AFSCs per promotion cycle, given small sample sizes in many AFSCs. Although the relative influence of each factor changed somewhat across years for each AFSC, the overall pattern of results regarding the range and median influence of each factor were similar to our findings when we collapsed data across promotion cycles. Therefore, for ease of interpretation, we report the results when the data were collapsed across promotion cycles.

Figure 4.1. Boxplots of the Percentage of Relative Influence of WAPS Factors on Promotions Across AFSCs

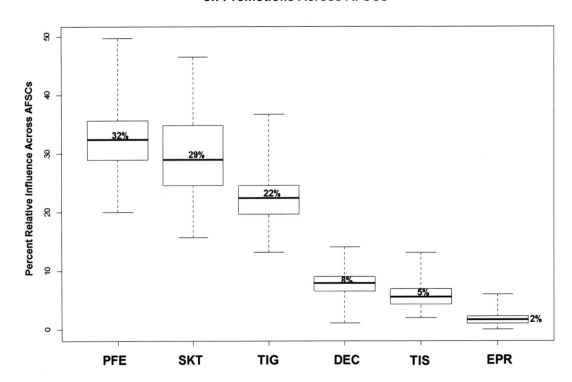

NOTES: The whiskers of each boxplot in the figure show the minimum and maximum relative influence of the WAPS factor across AFSCs, while the middle box shows the interquartile range (middle 50 percent of observations). The lower edge of the box represents the 25th percentile, the top edge of the box represents the 75th percentile, and the center line represents the median relative influence across AFSCs. DEC=decorations.

Most importantly, though, consistent with findings from our interviews, for all AFSCs, the PFE, SKT, and TIG have a greater influence than decorations, TIS, and EPR. In fact, these three factors account for 83 percent of the median influence of who gets promoted across AFSCs. Of particular note, the EPR factor, which is intended to measure job performance, has only a 2-percent median influence on promotion outcomes to master sergeant across AFSCs.

As shown in Table 4.1, the main reason the EPR has such little influence is that the mean EPR score for eligible airmen is 134 out of 135 points, with little deviation from the mean. In fact, data show that 84 percent of all airmen eligible for promotion to master sergeant had perfect EPR scores in WAPS. Although some restriction in the range of EPR scores may be expected by the time airmen reach higher ranks, this little variance in true scores is unlikely. Thus, the EPR— the main method intended to measure past performance and assess key procedural knowledge and skills as well as motivation—does not do a good job of differentiating among those airmen eligible for promotion to master sergeant.

Table 4.1. Score Distributions on WAPS Factors

WAPS Factor	Maximum Possible Points	Mean Score	Standard Deviation
SKT	100	54	12
PFE	100	55	12
TIS	40	35	5
TIG	60	27	7
Decorations	25	11	5
EPR	135	134	4

As Figure 4.2 shows, although the EPR accounts for the largest percentage of total possible points for promotion to master sergeant (29 percent), it has only a 2-percent influence on promotion outcomes to master sergeant across AFSCs. In contrast, the PFE, SKT, and TIG end up having a much greater influence than intended.

Figure 4.2. Intended and Actual Relative Influence of WAPS Factors

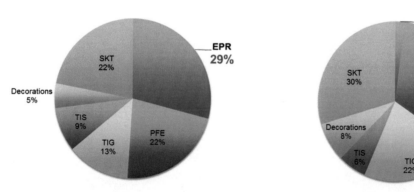

Percentage of Points in the
Weighted Airman Promotion System

Mean Percentage Influence on master sergeant
Promotion Outcomes Across AFSCs

Summary

The current WAPS factors have the potential to either directly or indirectly measure key declarative knowledge, procedural knowledge and skills, and motivation important to fulfilling the increased leadership responsibilities of a master sergeant in the Air Force. Specifically, the SKT and PFE are intended to provide direct measures of important declarative knowledge. TIS and TIG likely provide some degree of indirect or proxy measure of declarative and procedural knowledge and skills, although they are likely to be less relevant as measures for leadership potential as a master sergeant if technical sergeants have not had any supervisory opportunities.

The EPR and decorations scores have the potential to provide direct and indirect measures of key procedural knowledge and skills and motivation through an assessment of past performance.

Our analysis, however, found that one of the most important factors, the EPR (which measures past performance), has a relatively small influence on actual promotion outcomes due to little variance in EPR scores. As a result, promotions to the master sergeant rank are largely determined only by scores on knowledge tests (SKT and PFE) and TIG. Therefore, measures of important procedural knowledge and skills, motivation, and other characteristics are not captured under the current functioning of WAPS.

This finding is also consistent with previous RAND research (Schiefer et al., 2008) and evaluations of WAPS that have used a policy-capturing method similar to that used in the initial development of WAPS to capture the weights a promotion board would place on each factor. The most recent Air Force WAPS revalidation study recommended greater emphasis on job performance and less emphasis on longevity (Shore and Gould, 2004). The study authors note that, "the EPR score does not distinguish between the average performer and the top performer, and in some cases, it doesn't distinguish between the 25th percentile performer and the 99th percentile performer" (p. 28).

These findings also seem to be consistent with larger perceptions of WAPS in the Air Force, with our interview participants raising concerns that performance and leadership potential are not adequately assessed in determining who gets promoted to master sergeant. Based on these findings, we conclude that the current promotion system is not effectively assessing key KSAOs or leadership potential needed to successfully perform as a master sergeant in the Air Force.

5. Options for Improvement

In this chapter, we identify and assess options for improving how the current promotion process assesses master sergeant leadership potential in the Air Force. Based on our findings in Chapter Four, the most obvious course of action is to revise the EPR to better differentiate performance and thus potential as a master sergeant. Another is to include additional factors in WAPS to provide a better assessment of leadership potential. We evaluate both of these options in the following sections.

Improving the Performance Evaluation System

When measured accurately, past performance is one of the best predictors of future performance, as described in Chapter Four. The EPR, which is intended to measure performance, also provides a format for assessing a range of skills and abilities important to fulfilling the increased leadership responsibilities of a master sergeant in the Air Force. However, like many organizations, the Air Force struggles with accurately differentiating among levels of job performance for airmen. Research finds that similar issues with rater inflation are prevalent among many organizations beyond the Air Force and particularly occur when raters face conflicting goals, such as wanting to identify the best performers with the potential to be promoted while also wanting to motivate and maintain positive relationships with subordinates (Kozlowski, Chao, and Morrison, 1998). In our interviews, many respondents noted that even if they did not feel the airman deserved the highest score, they did not want to hurt his or her chances for future promotion, particularly when they knew everyone else was receiving high ratings.

Research on effective performance evaluation practices points to several steps that organizations can take to try to promote accurate performance ratings (Arvey and Murphy, 1998; Murphy and Cleveland, 1995; Kozlowski, Chao, and Morrison, 1998; and Newman, Kinney, and Farr, 2004). For example, Murphy and Cleveland (1995) highlight the five following important conditions for accurate ratings (p. 265):

- Good and poor performances are clearly defined.
- The principle of distinguishing among workers in terms of their levels of performance is widely accepted.
- There is a high degree of trust in the system.
- Low ratings do not automatically result in the loss of valued rewards.
- Value rewards are clearly linked to accuracy in performance appraisal.

Research building on these conditions further suggests that increasing the level of rater accountability may improve the accuracy of ratings. This includes ensuring there is clear support from senior leadership and consistency across units in discouraging inflation. Research also finds that raters are more likely to make accurate judgments about performance when they have to justify their ratings in writing (Mero and Motowidlo, 1995; Mero, Motowidlo, and Anna, 2003). Finally, another well-documented strategy for improving the accuracy of performance evaluations is through the use of frame-of-reference training, which ensures that all raters share common conceptualizations of performance dimensions and different levels of performance (Roch, Woehr, Mishra, and Kieszczynska, 2012).

However, inflation in performance evaluations is a long-standing issue in the Air Force and it may be difficult to completely eliminate inflation of EPR scores, given the immense cultural shift that would be required. Although similar inflation problems have led other organizations to adopt forced distributions or rankings to ensure variance in performance evaluations, such a system must be implemented with caution as it can also result in unintended negative consequences (see Lawler, 2002; Pfeffer and Sutton, 2006a; 2006b). In particular, the use of forced performance rankings can lead to perceptions of unfairness in the evaluation system, resulting in lower morale. It can also foster a more competitive environment, which can be particularly detrimental for organizations that thrive on teamwork and collaboration. Comparing airmen across different MAJCOMs, squadrons, and work units can also be problematic. For example, the middle performer in one squadron may actually have more leadership potential than a top performer in another squadron, but this might go unnoticed because of different comparison groups within each squadron.

Thus, we recommend the Air Force pursue the aforementioned evidence-based improvements in their evaluation system in an effort to promote more accurate performance evaluations and to prevent inflation. However, due to the potential challenges in fully eliminating rating inflation, we also recommend that the Air Force consider additional measures of leadership potential that may be included in WAPS.

Additional Assessment Methods for Inclusion in WAPS

Next, we provide an overview of the some of the most widely researched assessment methods available for selecting and promoting job candidates, and we evaluate the extent to which each method may improve the ability of WAPS to assess leadership potential of master sergeant candidates. Our selection, although not comprehensive, was guided by expert knowledge of available methods for personnel selection and promotion. Consequently, we did not review assessment methods found to be poor predictors of performance (e.g., handwriting analysis known as graphology). Additionally, we did not include cognitive ability tests in our overview because the Air Force currently measures job knowledge in WAPS, and job knowledge is directly related to cognitive ability (therefore, adding a cognitive ability test would provide little value). In short, the assessments reviewed in the next sections all have the potential to provide incremental value to the current promotion system. Some of the assessment tools reviewed are designed to measure a specific construct or skill (e.g., personality) whereas other methods can be customized to measure a broad range of KSAOs most relevant to an organization or position.

We evaluate the trade-offs of these different methods to assess which might be best suited to improving the ability of the current promotion system to select airmen who will be able to fulfill the increased leadership responsibilities of a master sergeant in the Air Force, while at the same time weighing other factors important to the Air Force in implementing any changes. In evaluating each assessment method, we used the following criteria:

- measurement of attributes: the extent to which the assessment method is able to assess a range of leadership attributes (i.e., KSAOs) relevant to predicting performance as a master sergeant in the Air Force
- validity: research evidence on the operational validity of each assessment method (i.e., typical relationship between the predictor and job performance)
- diversity: research evidence on the extent to which the assessment method may have an adverse impact on minority promotion[1]
- cost: additional cost to the Air Force to develop and/or implement the assessment method
- fairness perceptions: the extent to which airmen are likely to perceive the assessment method as a fair assessment of their potential.

We first list the extent to which each assessment method measures attributes relevant to predicting performance as a master sergeant in the Air Force and validity, as these are the most important or necessary criteria. Based on the goals of the Air Force, we then include the impact on diversity, cost, and fairness perceptions (although these are listed in no particular order of importance). We present greater details on our analysis and specific research findings related to these criteria for each assessment method in Appendix E.

It is important to note that the research presented in this overview is based primarily on quantitative summaries that integrated results across many individual studies (i.e., meta-analyses). Therefore, the results we review represent typical or average results, and each assessment method may function differently within WAPS. For example, only candidates meeting specific criteria (e.g., TIS) are eligible for promotion in WAPS, which may create more

---

[1] Adverse or disparate impact exists when an employment practice that is not intended to discriminate has an adverse effect on members of a particular race, ethnicity, religion, sex, or national origin. For example, adverse impact would be said to exist when a particular promotion factor results in fewer women being promoted than men. A common rule of thumb for measuring the existence of adverse impact is the four-fifths rule, which says that adverse impact is considered present when an employment practice results in the proportion of applicants that are selected or promoted from a protected group being less than four-fifths (80 percent) of the proportion of applicants selected or promoted from the group with the highest selection rate. For more information, see Equal Employment Opportunity Commission, 1978.

range restriction on assessments measuring supervisory experience (e.g., biodata). In other words, a meta-analysis is a useful guide to identify potential measures. However, a well-executed validation study would need to be conducted to identify the true operational validity and potential adverse impact for any assessment method used in WAPS.

Personality Tests

The first assessment method we evaluated, a personality test, is actually not a method in itself but a common predictor of job performance. As described in Chapter Two, research has shown that the Big-Five dimensions of personality are related to a variety of important outcomes, including task performance, contextual performance (e.g., helping others), and, most importantly, leadership (Barrick and Mount, 1991; Bono and Judge, 2004; Chiaburu et al., 2011; Judge, Bono et al., 2002). The strength of the relationship varies, however, depending on which personality dimension is examined and which outcome variable is measured (Barrick and Mount, 1991), with personality tests being the most predictive of performance when combinations of relevant personality dimensions are examined (Judge, Bono, et al., 2002).

Currently, personality is not directly measured by any of the WAPS factors. Personality tests also have the advantage of being fairly low in cost and require little time to administer or score given that they are traditionally multiple-choice tests that can be administered by paper-and-pencil or over a computer. Additionally, they are less likely to result in adverse impact for minority groups compared to other assessment methods (Foldes, Duehr, and Ones, 2008).

Despite these advantages, several concerns often deter organizations from implementing personality measures for selection or promotion. The most widely held concern is that job candidates can and will fake their responses on a personality inventory. Indeed, this issue "has been one of the greatest challenges to the Army's ability to implement and sustain the operational, large-scale use of self-report personality measures, especially in high-stakes testing situations" (White et al., 2008, p. 291). While some studies have shown that the "faking problem" may be overstated (Hogan, Barrett, and Hogan, 2007), others have shown how fakers can rise to the top of the score distribution and may have a greater chance of being selected than nonfakers (Mueller-Hanson, Heggestad, and Thornton, 2003). In addition, job candidates tend to rate the acceptability of personality tests slightly lower than other personnel selection measures (Anderson, Salgado, and Hulsheger, 2010), and it is unclear how well job candidates competing for promotion would react to taking a personality test.

Although personality tests are not the best tool for measuring technical skills (e.g., budgeting), they are very effective for measuring important traits associated with interpersonal and management skills (e.g., leading and managing teams). Further, research shows that personality is related to job performance as well as leadership effectiveness; however, the potential benefits of using a traditional personality test for promotion may be limited by their acceptability or perceived fairness and the extent that candidates are motivated to fake their responses. Furthermore, there are alternative methods for measuring personality, including a structured interview and situational judgment tests, which we will discuss later.

Biodata Inventories

Biodata inventories are self-report measures similar to an application blank that are designed to assess relevant dimensions from a person's life history (e.g., the year an individual was first provided with supervision responsibilities), which can then be linked to future job performance. Despite the emphasis on historical events, biodata measures have often incorporated questions that also measure respondents' personality or behavioral tendencies (e.g., what would you do if . . . ?). Therefore, a biodata inventory could be designed for a specific organization to match the important performance dimensions identified in a job analysis. Thus, custom-designed inventories could be used to predict a number of interpersonal, leadership, and technical skills identified in Chapter Two.

Overall, research has shown that biodata measures tend to be very good indicators of future performance (Schmidt and Hunter, 1998). They also have, depending on item content, relatively low to moderate adverse impact for minorities (Bobko and Roth, 2013). Additionally, they can be given in hard-copy form or over a computer, requiring little cost or time to administer or score.

However, as a self-report measure, concerns have been raised that job candidates will distort or inflate their responses, like personality tests. Research suggests that using verifiable items may be less susceptible to faking and may have higher relationships with job performance (Harold, McFarland, and Weekley, 2006; Lefkowitz et al., 1999). These concerns about potential faking may result in some perceptions of unfairness, but research suggests that, in general, job candidates react somewhat favorably toward biodata measures (Anderson et al., 2010). It is also important to note that some of what could be included as part of a biodata measure could also be assessed through nonself-report methods, such as through a promotion board review of personnel records reflecting career and education histories.

Interviews

Employment interviews are among the most frequently used methods to hire job candidates (Schmidt and Zimmerman, 2004) and can be developed to measure a wide range of KSAOs. For example, interviews have been designed to assess personality (e.g., conscientiousness), leadership skills, experience, training, and occupational interests. Therefore, the Air Force could design interview questions to measure a range of the KSAOs identified in Chapter Two that are not currently measured by the other WAPS factors, including a candidate's ability to effectively perform any of the important duties (e.g., leading and managing teams and managing resources). Interviews also receive very positive reactions from job candidates, due in part to having an opportunity to demonstrate their qualities (Anderson et al., 2010). Furthermore, interviews have been shown to have relatively low adverse impact for minorities (Bobko and Roth, 2013).

Several meta-analyses have been conducted on the validity of the employment interview and have consistently shown that interviews can be a good indicator of future performance (Huffcutt and Woehr, 1999; Krajewski et al., 2006; McDaniel Whetzel, et al., 1994; Taylor and Small, 2002; Wiesner and Cronshaw, 1988). However, there is variability in validity estimates depending on the degree of structure, type of question, and KSAOs measured. First, highly structured interviews tend to produce much higher correlations with job performance compared to unstructured interviews (McDaniel, Whetzel, et al., 1994; Wiesner and Cronshaw, 1988).[2] Interviews that use behavior-based questions (e.g., describe a time when you had to . . .) compared to situational-based questions (e.g., what would you do . . . ?) also tend to have higher validity.[3]

The primary limiting factor in utilizing interviews as part of a promotion system is the high cost and time required to conduct interviews with individual candidates for promotion. Thus, although ubiquitous in private organizations, interviews are not widely used in military promotion systems.

Work Samples

Appropriately named, work sample tests can be defined as "a hands-on performance test in which a job applicant or employee is required to actually perform a job-related task under the same conditions as those required on the job" (Callinan and Robertson, 2000, p. 248). For example, a work sample test for a mechanic might have a candidate assess and fix a problem using a real engine and tools. As Callinan and Robertson (2000) note, work sample tests can vary considerably in design. First, they can vary in the extent to which they sample or incorporate relevant tasks from the target job. A broad bandwidth work sample would require job candidates to perform a majority of the critical tasks for the position being considered whereas a narrow bandwidth work sample may only include a small subset of tasks from the target job. The bandwidth considered in designing a work sample is often determined by cost and time restrictions. As more of the target job is sampled, test administration time and costs will increase. A second characteristic of work samples, fidelity, refers to the likeness of the test content to the job in both the types of tasks performed on the test and the mode of response (e.g., multiple choice vs. open-ended written). For example, a work sample that requires candidates to select from a list of solutions to a work problem would have a low level of fidelity, whereas a test

---

[2] A structured interview provides the same questions and scores similar responses in the same way for every candidate. Recent research, however, highlighting concerns with applicant acceptability of highly structured interviews, suggests that unstructured interviews can be combined to produce validity equal to that of a single structured interview (Schmidt and Zimmerman, 2004). That is, it may be possible to produce a reliable score for a job candidate by combining three to four separate unstructured interviews.
[3] Research comparing these question formats show a slight favor in one study for behavioral-based questions compared to situational-based questions (Taylor and Small, 2002); however, larger differences still favoring behavior-based questions emerged in a more recent study that focused specifically on managerial performance (Krajewski et al., 2006).

requiring candidates to write a written response in a memo would have a higher level of fidelity. A third distinguishing feature among work sample tests is the type of tasks that candidates perform. Work sample tests can be designed to have candidates engage in interpersonal interactions (e.g., delegating tasks in a role play), provide written responses (e.g., emails), and perform hands-on technical tasks (e.g., repairing equipment). Therefore, a work sample could be designed to measure the key procedural skills not currently assessed in WAPS by assessing how well candidates would perform in simulations of key master sergeant duties identified in Chapter Two. In other words, it could measure whether they are able to actually apply some of the declarative knowledge measured by the SKT and PFE.

Previous meta-analyses have indicated strong support for the validity of work sample tests in predicting job performance (Roth, Bobko et al., 2008; Schmidt and Hunter, 1998). Work sample tests are also typically well-received by job candidates and have been found to have the highest overall favorability ratings compared to other popular personnel selection methods (Anderson et al., 2010).

Like interviews, however, the primary limiting factor in utilizing works samples is the cost and time required to conduct works samples with individual candidates for promotion. These can become especially significant as the bandwidth of the work sample expands to cover more tasks relevant to the job. In addition, work sample tests are usually intended for candidates who already have experience in the target job. Therefore, a work sample may be better for measuring application of technical expertise in each AFSC instead of for measuring the potential to take on new or complex supervisory or resource management activities, for example.

Assessment Centers

Assessment centers are among the most popular methods for selecting and developing leaders in private organizations and are typically well received by applicants (Macan et al., 1994). An assessment center is a collection of tests (i.e., assessments), in which multiple raters (i.e., assessors) measure multiple KSAOs. Furthermore, for it to be a true assessment center, one of the tests/assessments must be a work-related simulation (i.e., work sample). For example, an assessment center might require candidates to take a job knowledge test, participate in an interview, and engage in a series of role-play simulations (e.g., in-basket exercise).[4] During each simulation, trained assessors observe and evaluate the job candidates' performance. Recent meta-analyses indicate that assessment centers have among the highest correlations with job performance (Arthur et al., 2003; Bowler and Woehr, 2006; Meriac et al., 2008).

Since assessment centers can be customized for a specific organization and position, a job analysis is often used to guide development to ensure that important job duties and skills are

---

[4] In-basket exercises, among the most widely used simulations, may involve a candidate responding to "an accumulation of memos, reports, notes of incoming telephone calls, letters, and other materials supposedly collected in the in-basket of a job he or she is to take over" (Howard, 1974, p. 118). Other simulations may involve group problem–solving exercises, leaderless group discussions, and individual presentations or briefings.

being assessed. This customization provides organizations the flexibility to measure a variety of KSAOs. Therefore, the Air Force could integrate any of the important master sergeant job duties or skills (e.g., leadership, communication) into an assessment center.

Although assessment centers are clearly valuable tools for assisting organizations in selecting and developing leaders, they, again, require considerable investments of cost, personnel, and time. These factors would likely make an assessment center for master sergeant promotion impractical at this time.

Situational Judgment Tests

As previously discussed, assessment centers and work samples are potentially very good methods for identifying leadership potential for a specific role (e.g., a master sergeant in the Air Force). Although these carefully constructed simulations are typically well received by candidates, they are very expensive to develop and implement. Research suggests that the benefits of a simulation approach can be captured at lower cost through a multiple-choice test known as a situational judgment test (SJT) (Motowidlo, Dunnette, and Carter, 1990; Motowidlo and Tippins, 1993). SJT items measure the effectiveness of candidates' judgments about appropriate courses of action in response to different job-related problems or dilemmas. As a result, SJTs can be designed to measure a wide range of KSAOs related to performance in a specific job or position.

Furthermore, the research evidence from meta-analyses is quite positive regarding the predictive validity of SJTs (Christian, Edwards, and Bradley, 2010; McDaniel, Morgeson, et al., 2001). In fact, a recent quantitative review of KSAOs measured by SJTs indicated that tests that measure leadership and interpersonal skills can be very effective predictors of overall job performance (Christian et al., 2010). Additionally, leadership SJTs were found to be relatively good indicators of managerial performance, and tend to produce relatively low to moderate adverse impact (Bobko and Roth, 2013).[5]

Within a military context, the U.S. Army Research Institute for the Behavioral and Social Sciences has examined the benefits of an SJT in its evaluation on several potential predictors of Army NCO performance (Knapp et al., 2002). Their SJT was developed to measure representative KSAOs in several areas, including supervising subordinates, team leadership, cultural tolerance, motivating others, and problem-solving. More recently, the Air Force has been developing an SJT that will be included as part of the Air Force Officer Qualifying Test (AFOQT) in junior officer selection. Implementation of the newly developed SJT is planned for 2014.

Overall, SJTs can measure KSAOs not already covered by other WAPS factors, and they have been found to have incremental validity over cognitive ability measures (McDaniel, Hartman, et al., 2007). Furthermore, compared to other assessments we reviewed, the flexibility

---

[5] However, research indicates that the level of adverse impact may vary depending on which KSAOs are measured.

and specificity provided by an SJT, in addition to the relatively low cost to develop and implement it, would likely make this method of assessment a valuable addition to the master sergeant promotion process.

Promotion Board Ratings

Finally, we evaluated the inclusion of a master sergeant promotion board. A promotion board score was originally included as a factor in WAPS for promotion to E-4 through E-7 when it was developed. However, a 1969 field test of WAPS with the Alaskan Air Command found that when excluding the board score, the composite score gave airmen the same relative ranking as it would have under the traditional board evaluation process. Therefore, when WAPS was established in 1970, it did not contain a board score as one of the factors for promotion to E-4 through E-7. WAPS developers were not able to develop a similar composite score that mirrored a traditional board evaluation for promotion to E-8 and E-9, however, and SNCOs felt that the selection board evaluation provided the best means of assessing the management and supervisory capacity of E-8 and E-9 promotion candidates. Therefore, a board score remains a large factor in promotion to the other SNCO grades.[6] Since the development of WAPS, however, there have been significant changes in force size, operational requirements, and airmen responsibilities, with concern that greater leadership responsibility and authority is being pushed down to lower levels. The inclusion of a promotion board, similar to that used for promotion to the SNCO ranks of E-8 and E-9, may be helpful in selecting airmen who will be able to fulfill these increased leadership responsibilities as a master sergeant.

All of the other services also use some variation of a board process to determine promotion to E-7.[7] Both the Army and Marine Corps conduct centralized promotion boards for promotion to E-7, with recent Army boards reviewing roughly 38,000 records for promotion-eligible soldiers, and the Marine Corps reviewing roughly 5,400 records for promotion-eligible Marines. The Navy also conducts a centralized promotion board, but this is used as part of a hurdle system in which all eligible sailors first receive an overall score that is based on their results on a Navy-wide advancement exam along with past duty-performance and conduct evaluations. Sailors are then rank-ordered, with only the top 60 percent going forward to a selection board. This results in roughly 18,000 records being reviewed for promotion to E-7 in the Navy.

As described in Chapter Three, current boards for promotion to E-8 and E-9 in the Air Force are intended to consider performance, leadership, breadth of experience, job responsibility, professional competence, specific achievements, and education in determining their rating. They review the following documents:

- all EPRs for the past ten years

---

[6] See Shore and Gould (2004) for a more detailed discussion.

[7] The information regarding the processes used in the other services was obtained through interviews with various service representatives in charge of managing various parts of the promotion process.

- citations for all decorations
- SNCO Evaluation Brief (a computer-generated snapshot of the airman's career)
- Article 15/Nonjudicial Punishment (if applicable and determined to be filed by appropriate commander)
- record of courts-martial
- Air Force Form 77 (a letter of evaluation when a full completed EPR was not available due to breaks in service, EPR appeals, administrative correction, etc.).

Findings from our exploratory interviews indicate that a board may also offer a means to assess aspects of technical sergeant performance that are meant to be captured with the EPR factor score. Interview participants indicated that although many airmen receive a perfect overall evaluation (the score used to calculate the EPR factor score in WAPS), supervisors often communicate additional information through their markdowns and narrative comments on specific performance categories. Additionally, E-8 and E-9 board scores have considerable variance across airmen, suggesting that they may provide a similar opportunity to differentiate among airmen eligible for promotion to master sergeant.

Almost no published research exists on the validity of board ratings for selection or promotion of job candidates. One exception is the recent implementation of a new promotion system by the Royal Canadian Mounted Police (Catano, Darr, and Campbell, 2007). The primary purpose of this review board was to resolve discrepancies when supervisors and candidates disagreed on their performance ratings and to "control for supervisors who may give uniformly high or uniformly low ratings, and to achieve consistency of supervisory ratings across candidates" (Catano et al., 2007, p. 209). The three-member board was given the authority to change a score, but first it had to reach consensus, then follow up with a written justification for the change. To evaluate the effectiveness of the promotion system, board ratings were correlated with future promotions to higher ranks. Overall, the board ratings were moderate predictors of future promotions, with somewhat stronger correlations with promotions at lower ranks.

Although research has yet to fully examine the validity of a promotion board in the scientific sense, well-established guidelines for developing a reliable and valid board process can be leveraged from research on assessment centers and structured interviews. A review board also provides the additional advantage of having job candidates being independently evaluated by individuals of a higher rank, other than just the immediate supervisor. Therefore, a board could be designed to evaluate performance on the critical KSAOs needed to be successful as a master sergeant. Furthermore, from a fairness perspective, individuals expect their performance to be taken into account when making promotion selections. A promotion board provides this opportunity and is likely to be accepted by airmen given its use for promotion to E-8 and E-9 ranks.

The main challenge to holding a master sergeant promotion board would be the additional cost. Consistent with this potential limitation, 52 percent of our interview participants expressed concerns regarding the logistics of holding a master sergeant promotion board, particularly in terms of the cost and large number of records that would have to be reviewed. Similar concerns regarding board logistics were voiced by Air Force Personnel Center (AFPC) representatives in charge of executing WAPS and by representatives from the Selection Board Secretariat, who are responsible for organizing the officer and enlisted promotion boards. We explore the potential additional cost that a promotion board may create in the next section.

Cost of a Master Sergeant Promotion Board

Currently, senior master sergeant boards review approximately 13,000 eligible records each year, and the process takes three weeks.[8] The board is comprised of 14 panels chaired by a brigadier general. Each panel is staffed with one colonel and two chief master sergeants. In addition, the board requires support from seven senior master sergeant administrative assistants.

There are approximately 60 percent more eligible master sergeant records in a given year, or approximately 21,000 annually. This increased caseload would require an increase in either the number of panels, the length of the board process, or both (relative to what is currently used for senior master sergeant boards). While the costs would be nearly identical regardless of which option is chosen to meet staffing needs, we fixed the time commitment to three weeks with the assumption that additional time away from their home station assignment would be difficult. Consequently, this approach would require additional panels to be staffed, resulting in an estimated total of 22 panels for a master sergeant board. Based on the estimated staffing needs, the number of personnel and the total opportunity cost expressed in days away from primary duty for a master sergeant board is presented in Table 5.1. We provide greater details on our cost estimates in Appendix F.

---

[8] Chief master sergeant boards review between 2,000 and 3,000 records and take two weeks to conduct.

Table 5.1. Personnel and Total Days Away from Primary Duty by Pay Grade

	Master Sergeant Administrative Assistants	Chief Master Sergeants	Colonels	Brigadier Generals
Number of personnel	11	44	22	1
Total required days	165	660	330	15

It is important to note that the relative value of these days is difficult to determine. To what extent does a brigadier general wing commander's absence affect the completion of his or her duties and the wing's operation, as compared to a senior master sergeant section chief's absence from a wing?

There will also be monetary costs for the travel and per diem of board members, as well as records maintenance and preparation. Estimates of these annual costs are presented in Table 5.2.

Table 5.2. Estimated Annual Costs for Master Sergeant Promotion Board

Travel/ Transportation	Per Diem	Records Maintenance	Total Cost
$66,300	$279,240	$975,000	$1,320,540

As shown in Tables 5.1 and 5.2, there are significant annual opportunity and monetary costs associated with holding a board to review all master sergeant records. Additionally, representatives from the Selection Board Secretariat, who are responsible for organizing the promotion boards, expressed concerns regarding the space of facilities and scheduling for such a large board.

A potential option for dealing with the seemingly prohibitive nature of holding a promotion board that would review all 21,000 records is to have a hurdle system to limit the number of records that go to the boards, similar to the system used by the Navy. For the Air Force, such a hurdle system could be created by using the other WAPS scores (i.e., PFE, SKT, TIS, TIG, decorations, EPR) to rank-order promotion-eligible individuals within each AFSC. Then, only the records for a portion of the top candidates from each rank-ordered list would be sent to a board for scoring (e.g., top 50 percent), reducing resource requirements to the size of an E-8 board.

It is also important to note that AFPC recently implemented the electronic Board Operations Support System (eBOSS). When implemented as planned, this electronic system will reduce the staff and time needed to maintain and prepare records for board consideration. Because eBoss takes advantage of records available in the Air Force's electronic records system, the Automated Records Management System (ARMS), the personnel who maintain the paper records will no longer be needed. In addition, administrative assistants will no longer be required. These reduced resource requirements further reduce the financial cost of holding promotion boards.

Tables 5.3 and 5.4 show the reduction in opportunity and monetary costs for a master sergeant promotion board using a hurdle system with 50 percent of records and the addition of eBOSS.

Table 5.3. Days Away from Primary Duty—Totals for Promotion Board Options

Percentage of Records Reviewed	Chief Master Sergeants	Colonels	Brigadier Generals
100% of records	660	330	15
50% of records	420	210	15

Table 5.4. Costs for Promotion Board Options (Travel, Transportation, Per Diem, Records Maintenance)

Percentage of Records Reviewed	Paper Records Total Cost	eBOSS Total Cost
100% of records	$1,320,540	$314,530
50% of records	$728,500	$190,490

Thus, the use of a hurdle system to reduce the number of records to be reviewed along with the implementation of eBOSS greatly reduces both the opportunity costs and monetary costs of holding a master sergeant board.

Summary

There are pros and cons to all of the assessment methods we evaluated. Overall, adding an SJT and board ratings as additional factors in WAPS seem most promising. Although other predictors we reviewed were shown to have acceptable levels of validity, some predictors are not able to assess as wide a range of KSAOs (e.g., personality tests) or would be difficult to administer due to high costs and excessive time requirements (e.g., assessment centers and interviews). Others also raise concerns about potential acceptability (e.g., faking on personality tests). In contrast, SJTs are relatively inexpensive and could measure a range of important leadership KSAOs not currently assessed by existing WAPS factors. Although more expensive, the addition of a board rating process also has the potential to increase the breadth of KSAOs examined by measuring past performance. Furthermore, the integration of a hurdle system can reduce costs by requiring the board to review only a portion of the top candidates (e.g., top 50 percent based on WAPS scores). Additionally, the transition from paper to electronic records (i.e., eBOSS) further decreases the costs associated with a board process. In conclusion, the addition of an SJT and a board is expected to increase the likelihood of promoting airmen who will be successful master sergeants; however, any changes to WAPS should be evaluated in a follow-on validation study to determine the utility of adding these new measures.

6. Conclusion and Recommendations

The goal of this study was to examine and provide recommendations for improving the promotion process to master sergeant. Since its establishment in 1970, WAPS and its underlying factors have remained largely unchanged. However, with recent deployments, increased joint operations, and changes in force size and the general operational environment, there is concern that more responsibility and authority is being pushed down to NCOs. As the first level of senior enlisted leadership, the ability of master sergeants to be effective leaders is especially critical. A key component in ensuring that airmen serving as master sergeants have the required knowledge, skills, abilities, and other characteristics to fulfill the required leadership duties is having an effective promotion system for selecting airmen with the greatest potential to move from the rank of technical sergeant to master sergeant.

Our analysis found that, taken together, the current WAPS factors could ideally measure many of the key KSAOs identified as important for leadership as a master sergeant. However, we found that three out of the six WAPS factors account for the vast majority of variance in who gets promoted (83 percent of the median relative influence of who gets promoted across AFSCs): the SKT, PFE, and TIG. Of particular note, the EPR factor, which is intended to measure job performance, has only a 2-percent median relative influence on actual promotions across AFSCs. We found that it has little influence because there is little variance in EPR scores compared to other factors, with a mean EPR score of 134 out of 135 points for all airmen eligible for promotion to master sergeant. Thus, current promotion outcomes are largely based only on assessments of knowledge and tenure. The current promotion system is not effectively assessing other critical procedural knowledge and skills and other characteristics needed to successfully fulfill the additional leadership responsibilities of a master sergeant in the Air Force.

Based on these results, we explored potential options for addressing this gap. The most obvious option is to explore ways to revise the EPR to better assess technical sergeants' potential as master sergeants. However, data on EPR scores over the last several decades suggests that this is a long-standing issue and is deeply embedded in Air Force culture, making it potentially difficult to fully eliminate. Another avenue for addressing the gap in the current promotion system is to include additional factors in WAPS to better measure leadership potential as a master sergeant. We examined some of the most widely researched methods available for selecting and promoting job candidates, including a board process that is commonly used in the military, and evaluated the extent to which each method may improve WAPS's ability to assess leadership potential as a master sergeant, while balancing other factors important to the Air Force in implementing any changes.

Recommendations

Based on the study findings, we developed three overarching recommendations.

Examine the Validity and Utility of Implementing a Situational Judgment Test (SJT) and a Master Sergeant Promotion Board as Additional Measures of Leadership Potential

Based on our evaluation of additional measures that could be included in WAPS to better assess leadership potential as a master sergeant, a situational judgment test and promotion board seem to be particularly promising—and can complement each other by providing assessments of past performance, as well as how candidates are likely to handle future scenarios they may not have encountered as a technical sergeant.

Situational Judgment Test

As described previously, research suggests that the benefits of a simulation approach—one of the best methods for identifying leadership potential—can be captured at lower cost through a multiple-choice test known as a situational judgment test. SJT items, which measure the effectiveness of candidates' judgment about appropriate courses of action in response to different job-related problems or dilemmas, could even be included as part of current promotion testing (e.g., PFE or USAFSE). Ideally, the scenarios presented to candidates would reflect problems typically encountered by master sergeants in the Air Force. Similarly, the response options, which reflect effective and ineffective solutions, could be based on how master sergeants have attempted to handle these types of problems in the past. In doing so, they would increase the test's ability to predict candidates' performance and should increase candidates' acceptance of the test as a fair and useful assessment of leadership potential.

It is important to note, however, that there will need to be some time and resources put forth to developing an effective SJT as we have described. Recent development of an SJT for use as part of the AFOQT in junior officer selection required roughly six to nine months of work by a two-person team at the AFPC as part of their regular duties, and further validation of the instrument in terms of its relationship to performance was ongoing at the time of this study.

Overall, an SJT can measure KSAOs not already covered by other WAPS factors. Furthermore, the flexibility and specificity provided by an SJT, in addition to the relatively low cost to develop and implement it, would make this method of assessment a valuable addition to the master sergeant promotion system.

Promotion Board

In addition to an SJT, findings from our exploratory interviews indicate that a promotion board, such as those currently used for promotions to E-8 and E-9, may offer a means to assess performance as a technical sergeant in a number of domains and thus potential as a master sergeant. For example, although there is little variance in overall EPR scores, interview participants indicated that supervisors often communicate additional information through their markdowns and narrative comments on specific performance categories. From a fairness perspective, this is particularly important, given that individuals expect their performance to be taken into account for promotion. Promotion boards also have the ability to review a more holistic summary of each airman by examining the positions they have held in their careers, specific decorations earned, and any disciplinary actions.

As discussed previously, although published research has yet to fully examine the validity of a promotion board, well-established guidelines for establishing a reliable and valid board process can be leveraged from research on assessment centers and interviews. For example, it is critical that the board follow a structured rating process that includes specific criteria appropriate to evaluating a technical sergeant for promotion to the rank of master sergeant, including clearly defined performance levels (e.g., behaviorally anchored ratings scales). Additionally, promotion board procedures that are currently standard for E-8 and E-9 boards should be used. These include board members being trained on how to evaluate job candidates, policies for reconciling disagreements among raters, and a process for candidates to appeal the promotion decision.

Finally, to reduce costs and minimize any logistical challenges associated with holding a master sergeant board, we recommend the use of a hurdle system, so that only a portion of records would be sent to a board. One option for implementing a hurdle system is to first rank-order airmen within each AFSC using the current WAPS factors (SKT, PFE, TIS, TIG, decorations, EPR) and then send only a portion of the top airmen to a board (e.g., 50 percent). The board score could then be added back into the formula, similar to E-8 and E-9 promotions. Based on promotion rates, which have varied between 20 and 35 percent in recent years, a 50-percent cut-off guarantees that everyone promoted under the current system would still be reviewed by a board, while halving the number of records that a board would need to review, resulting in a board roughly the same size and duration as an E-8 promotion board. Ultimately, the Air Force may wish to be flexible as to the exact percentage of records sent to a board using the hurdle system depending on the promotion rate each year, while keeping in mind implications for utility. The board adds little value in distinguishing among airmen if too few records are reviewed, while costs and logistics may become difficult to manage if too many records are reviewed.

Assessment of Validity and Utility

Although we believe that both an SJT and a promotion board have the potential to improve the effectiveness of the current promotion process to master sergeant, we do not have data regarding the use of these assessment methods in the context of promoting Air Force technical sergeants to master sergeant and their potential relative contribution to WAPS. For example, although interview participants indicated that a promotion board would be able to better differentiate performance and potential based on the markdowns and narrative comments on specific performance categories of the EPR, further data is necessary to confirm this hypothesis in the context of promotion to master sergeant. Similarly, it is important to collect data to ensure that an SJT would improve the ability of the current system to select airmen that will perform well as a master sergeant beyond the current tests included in the promotion system.

Therefore, consistent with *Principles of the Validation and Use of Personnel Selection Procedures* (SIOP, 2003), we recommend first conducting a validation study with a sample of AFSCs to examine the contribution of a board and an SJT to WAPS in terms of the criteria outlined in Chapter Five (i.e., validity, diversity, fairness) prior to their use in determining actual promotion outcomes. Specifically, are scores on a situational judgment test (or a revised PFE, if the items are included in current testing) and promotion board good predictors of performance as a master sergeant in the Air Force (i.e., evidence of predictive validity)? Further, does the inclusion of these factors improve the overall validity of WAPS for master sergeant promotions? Addressing these questions provides the evidence needed to evaluate the costs and benefits (i.e., utility) of including these additional measures in WAPS. Additionally, a validation study is an important step in determining appropriate weights for each factor (i.e., range of points assigned to each factor). Finally, such a study can also examine and address any potential adverse impact on minorities or other fairness issues to ensure the new process will be accepted by airmen prior to full implementation.

Although there are several strategies for conducting a validation study, a concurrent validation strategy is one of the most cost-effective and efficient approaches. To conduct a concurrent validation study, scores need to be collected on both the predictor measures (i.e., SJT, WAPS factors) and the criterion measures (e.g., job performance assessments, EPRs, promotion board scores) from incumbent master sergeants. The incumbents included in the validation study should be representative of different AFSCs and other demographic variables (e.g., TIG, gender, race, age). Once the data have been collected, an analyst would compare the statistical relationship between WAPS factors and job performance criteria to ensure that each WAPS factor contributes incrementally to the prediction of master sergeant performance. If a WAPS factor is found not to predict performance, the measure should either be revised and further tested or eliminated from the model. For examining a promotion board, it would be possible to have boards score past records of master sergeants who would have been eligible for promotion in a given cycle from a sample of AFSCs to see how rankings for promotion may have changed, and to see the extent to which board scores predict performance as a master sergeant. AFSCs should be selected to represent different functional areas, while also ensuring that they are large enough in size to permit statistical analysis.

As described in Chapter Four, a lack of variance in performance evaluation ratings means there is currently no good measure of performance. This makes conducting the validation study, as well as any future evaluations of the promotion system, more difficult. Therefore, we also suggest the Air Force explore ways to collect performance data—for research purposes only that may be less inflated, given that scores collected only for research will not have any impact on an airman's career advancement opportunities.

Explore Ways to Improve the Enlisted Performance Evaluation Process Using
Evidence-Based Practices

It was beyond the scope of this study to fully review the current enlisted evaluation process and EPRs—and, as we acknowledged previously, it may be difficult to completely eliminate inflation of EPR scores given the immense cultural shift that would be required. However, we recommend that the Air Force explore potential improvements to the evaluation process in an effort to ensure that performance evaluations are as accurate as possible. Furthermore, a promotion board for master sergeants will only be as effective as the information available for board members to review. Therefore, it is critical that the EPR, which is the main source of information for the board, contain important and accurate information on performance that will be helpful in judging promotion potential.

To this end, key principles in effective performance evaluation, as described in Chapter Five, provide opportunities the Air Force can explore regarding the EPR and overall evaluation process (see Arvey and Murphy, 1998; Kozlowski et al., 1998; Murphy and Cleveland, 1995; and Newman, Kinney, and Farr, 2004). This includes reviewing the EPR form used for technical sergeants to ensure that it has clearly defined and specific performance dimensions that are relevant to the rank of technical sergeant and relevant to assessing potential as a master sergeant. Research also suggests that the performance dimensions being assessed should focus on judgments of observable employee behaviors, with a clear understanding of what constitutes successful and unsuccessful performance. If raters have different understandings of the performance dimensions, this can lead to lower reliability and accuracy in evaluations. Focusing on behaviors rather than individual characteristics also provides advantages, because behaviors are under individuals' control and provide a basis for feedback.

Continue to Periodically Reevaluate the Effectiveness of the Promotion System

Finally, we recommend that the Air Force continue to periodically reevaluate the effectiveness of the promotion system—not only for master sergeants but for all enlisted ranks. As there are changes to the operational environment, force size, and responsibilities at each rank, it is critical to examine whether WAPS is effective at identifying airmen with "the highest potential to fill positions of increased grade and responsibility" (U.S. Air Force, 2009c, p. 1). This evaluation should also include examining the extent to which current promotion factors are measuring key KSAOs predictive of performance at the next rank, the predictive validity of WAPS as a whole, and potential adverse impact on minorities.

Conclusion

As the size of the force and operational environment have changed, so to should the Air Force promotion system to ensure that airmen serving as master sergeants have the required knowledge, skills, abilities, and other characteristics to fulfill the necessary leadership responsibilities. Although the current promotion system has the potential to measure many of the key KSAOs our study identified as important for leadership as a master sergeant, promotion outcomes are driven by knowledge tests and TIG. Therefore, key procedural knowledge and skills, as well as motivation to lead and other characteristics important for successful performance as a master sergeant in the Air Force, are not being assessed. Our research identified two additional assessment methods: a promotion board and situational judgment test that we believe could improve the effectiveness of the current promotion system.

Appendix A. Enlisted Performance Report Forms

ENLISTED PERFORMANCE REPORT *(AB thru TSgt)*				
I. RATEE IDENTIFICATION DATA *(Refer to AFI 36-2406 for instructions on completing this form)*				
1. NAME *(Last, First, Middle Initial)*	2. SSN	3. GRADE		4. DAFSC
5. ORGANIZATION, COMMAND, LOCATION, AND COMPONENT			6. PAS CODE	7. SRID
8. PERIOD OF REPORT From: Thru:	9. NO. DAYS SUPERVISION		10. REASON FOR REPORT	

II. JOB DESCRIPTION

1. DUTY TITLE	2. SIGNIFICANT ADDITIONAL DUTY(S)

3. KEY DUTIES, TASKS, AND RESPONSIBILITIES   *(Limit text to 4 lines)*

III. PERFORMANCE ASSESSMENT

1. PRIMARY/ADDITIONAL DUTIES *(For SSgt/TSgt also consider Supervisory, Leadership and Technical Abilities)*

Consider Adapting, Learning, Quality, Timeliness, Professional Growth and Communication Skills *(Limit text to 4 lines)*

☐ Does Not Meet   ☐ Meets   ☐ Above Average   ☐ Clearly Exceeds

2. STANDARDS, CONDUCT, CHARACTER & MILITARY BEARING *(For SSgt/TSgt also consider Enforcement of Standards and Customs & Courtesies)*

Consider Dress & Appearance, Personal/Professional Conduct On/Off Duty   *(Limit text to 2 lines)*

☐ Does Not Meet   ☐ Meets   ☐ Above Average   ☐ Clearly Exceeds

3. FITNESS *(Maintains Air Force Physical Fitness Standards)* *(For referrals, limit text to 1 line)*

☐ Does Not Meet   ☐ Meets   ☐ Exempt

4. TRAINING REQUIREMENTS *(For SSgt/TSgt also consider PME, Off-duty Education, Technical Growth, Upgrade Training)*

Consider Upgrade, Ancillary, OJT and Readiness *(Limit text to 2 lines)*

☐ Does Not Meet   ☐ Meets   ☐ Above Average   ☐ Clearly Exceeds

5. TEAMWORK/FOLLOWERSHIP *(For SSgt/TSgt also consider Leadership, Team Accomplishments, Recognition/Reward Others)*

Consider Team Building, Support of Team, Followership *(Limit text to 2 lines)*

☐ Does Not Meet   ☐ Meets   ☐ Above Average   ☐ Clearly Exceeds

6. OTHER COMMENTS

Consider Promotion, Future Duty/Assignment/Education Recommendations and Safety, Security & Human Relations   *(Limit text to 2 lines)*

IV. RATER INFORMATION

NAME, GRADE, BR OF SVC, ORGN, COMMAND AND LOCATION	DUTY TITLE		DATE
	SSN	SIGNATURE	

AF FORM 910, 20080618   PREVIOUS EDITIONS ARE OBSOLETE   PRIVACY ACT INFORMATION: The information in this form is FOR OFFICIAL USE ONLY. Protect IAW the Privacy Act of 1974.

V. OVERALL PERFORMANCE ASSESSMENT
Overall Performance During Reporting Period

RATEE NAME:

ASSESSMENT	POOR (1)	NEEDS IMPROVEMENT (2)	AVERAGE (3)	ABOVE AVERAGE (4)	TRULY AMONG THE BEST (5)
RATER'S ASSESSMENT	☐	☐	☐	☐	☐
ADDITIONAL RATER'S ASSESSMENT	☐	☐	☐	☐	☐

Last feedback was performed on: _____   If feedback was not accomplished in accordance with AFI 36-2406, state the reason.

VI. ADDITIONAL RATER'S COMMENTS   (Limit text to 3 lines)   ☐ CONCUR   ☐ NON-CONCUR

NAME, GRADE, BR OF SVC, ORGN, COMMAND AND LOCATION	DUTY TITLE	DATE
	SSN SIGNATURE	

VII. FUNCTIONAL EXAMINER/AIR FORCE ADVISOR
(Indicate applicable review by marking the appropriate box.)   ☐ FUNCTIONAL EXAMINER   ☐ AIR FORCE ADVISOR

NAME, GRADE, BR OF SVC, ORGN, COMMAND AND LOCATION	DUTY TITLE	DATE
	SSN SIGNATURE	

VIII. UNIT COMMANDER/CIVILIAN DIRECTOR/OTHER AUTHORIZED REVIEWER   ☐ CONCUR   ☐ NON-CONCUR

NAME, GRADE, BR OF SVC, ORGN, COMMAND AND LOCATION	DUTY TITLE	DATE
	SSN SIGNATURE	

IX. RATEE'S ACKNOWLEDGEMENT

I understand my signature does not constitute agreement or disagreement. I acknowledge all required feedback was accomplished during the reporting period and upon receipt of this report.   ☐ Yes   ☐ No

SIGNATURE	DATE

INSTRUCTIONS

Complete this report IAW AFI 36-2406. Reports written by Colonels or civilians (GS-15 or higher, or Supervisory Pay Band 3), do not require an additional rater; however, endorsement by the rater's rater is permitted unless the report is written by a senior rater or the Chief Master Sergeant of the Air Force. When the rater's rater is not at least a MSgt or civilian (GS-07 or higher, or Supervisory Pay Band 1), the additional rater is the next official in the rating chain meeting grade requirements. An overall rating of 2 or negative comments require the EPR to be referred IAW AFI 36-2406. Rationale for any additional evaluator nonconcurring with an overall rating must be included. Section VIII Reviewer nonconcurrence must be included on an AF Form 77, Letter of Evaluation. If ratee is deployed, provide copy and feedback via e-mail/telecon.

PRIVACY ACT STATEMENT

AUTHORITY: Title 10 United States Code, Section 8013 and Executive Order 9397, 22 November 1943.

PURPOSE: Information is needed for verification of the individual's name and Social Security Number (SSN) as captured on the form at the time of rating.

ROUTINE USES: May specifically be disclosed outside the DoD as a routine use pursuant to 5 U.S.C. 552a(b)(3).

DISCLOSURE: Disclosure is mandatory; SSN is used for positive identification.

AF FORM 910, 20080618   PREVIOUS EDITIONS ARE OBSOLETE   PRIVACY ACT INFORMATION: The information in this form is FOR OFFICIAL USE ONLY. Protect IAW the Privacy Act of 1974.

ENLISTED PERFORMANCE REPORT (MSgt thru CMSgt)

I. RATEE IDENTIFICATION DATA (Refer to AFI 36-2406 for instructions on completing this form)

1. NAME (Last, First, Middle Initial)	2. SSN	3. GRADE	4. DAFSC

5. ORGANIZATION, COMMAND, LOCATION, AND COMPONENT	6. PAS CODE	7. SRID

8. PERIOD OF REPORT	9. NO. DAYS SUPERVISION	10. REASON FOR REPORT
From: Thru:		

II. JOB DESCRIPTION

1. DUTY TITLE	2. SIGNIFICANT ADDITIONAL DUTY(S)

3. KEY DUTIES, TASKS, AND RESPONSIBILITIES   (Limit text to 4 lines)

III. PERFORMANCE ASSESSMENT

1. PRIMARY DUTIES

Consider Quality, Quantity, Timeliness, Technical Knowledge, Leading, Managing and Supervising   (Limit text to 4 lines)

☐ Does Not Meet   ☐ Meets   ☐ Above Average   ☐ Clearly Exceeds

2. STANDARDS: ENFORCEMENT AND PERSONAL ADHERENCE, CONDUCT, CHARACTER, MILITARY BEARING & CUSTOMS AND COURTESIES

Consider Dress & Appearance, Personal/Professional Conduct On/Off Duty   (Limit text to 2 lines)

☐ Does Not Meet   ☐ Meets   ☐ Above Average   ☐ Clearly Exceeds

3. FITNESS (Maintains Air Force Physical Fitness Standards)   (For referrals, limit text to 1 line)

☐ Does Not Meet   ☐ Meets   ☐ Exempt

4. RESOURCE MANAGEMENT AND DECISION MAKING

Consider Efficiency, Judgment, Setting and Meeting Goals   (Limit text to 2 lines)

☐ Does Not Meet   ☐ Meets   ☐ Above Average   ☐ Clearly Exceeds

5. TRAINING, EDUCATION, OFF-DUTY EDUCATION, PME, PROFESSIONAL ENHANCEMENT AND COMMUNICATION

Consider Providing, Supporting and Personal Growth   (Limit text to 2 lines)

☐ Does Not Meet   ☐ Meets   ☐ Above Average   ☐ Clearly Exceeds

6. LEADERSHIP/TEAM BUILDING/FOLLOWERSHIP/MENTORSHIP

Consider Team Accomplishments, Leveraging Personal Experiences and Community Support, Recognition/Reward for Others   (Limit text to 2 lines)

☐ Does Not Meet   ☐ Meets   ☐ Above Average   ☐ Clearly Exceeds

7. OTHER COMMENTS

Consider Promotion, Future Duty/Assignment/Education Recommendations, Safety, Security & Human Relations   (Limit text to 2 lines)

IV. RATER INFORMATION

NAME, GRADE, BR OF SVC, ORGN, COMMAND AND LOCATION	DUTY TITLE		DATE
	SSN	SIGNATURE	

AF FORM 911, 20080618   PREVIOUS EDITIONS ARE OBSOLETE

PRIVACY ACT INFORMATION: The information in this form is FOR OFFICIAL USE ONLY. Protect IAW the Privacy Act of 1974.

V. OVERALL PERFORMANCE ASSESSMENT

Overall Performance During Reporting Period

RATEE NAME:

ASSESSMENT	POOR (1)	NEEDS IMPROVEMENT (2)	AVERAGE (3)	ABOVE AVERAGE (4)	TRULY AMONG THE BEST (5)
RATER'S ASSESSMENT	☐	☐	☐	☐	☐
ADDITIONAL RATER'S ASSESSMENT	☐	☐	☐	☐	☐

Last feedback was performed on: _____ If feedback was not accomplished in accordance with AFI 36-2406, state the reason.

VI. ADDITIONAL RATER'S COMMENTS *(Limit text to 3 lines)*   ☐ CONCUR   ☐ NON-CONCUR

NAME, GRADE, BR OF SVC, ORGN, COMMAND AND LOCATION	DUTY TITLE		DATE
	SSN	SIGNATURE	

VII. REVIEWER'S COMMENTS *(Limit text to 3 lines)*   ☐ CONCUR   ☐ NON-CONCUR

NAME, GRADE, BR OF SVC, ORGN, COMMAND AND LOCATION	DUTY TITLE		DATE
	SSN	SIGNATURE	

VIII. FINAL EVALUATORS POSITION
☐ SENIOR RATER
☐ SENIOR RATER'S DEPUTY
☐ INTERMEDIATE LEVEL
☐ LOWER LEVEL

IX. TIME-IN-GRADE ELIGIBLE
N/A for CMSgt or CMSgt Selectee
☐ N/A
☐ YES
☐ NO

X. FUNCTIONAL EXAMINER/AIR FORCE ADVISOR
(Indicate applicable review by marking the appropriate box)   ☐ FUNCTIONAL EXAMINER   ☐ AIR FORCE ADVISOR

NAME, GRADE, BR OF SVC, ORGN, COMMAND AND LOCATION	DUTY TITLE		DATE
	SSN	SIGNATURE	

XI. UNIT COMMANDER/CIVILIAN DIRECTOR/OTHER AUTHORIZED REVIEWER   ☐ CONCUR   ☐ NON-CONCUR

NAME, GRADE, BR OF SVC, ORGN, COMMAND AND LOCATION	DUTY TITLE		DATE
	SSN	SIGNATURE	

XII. RATEE'S ACKNOWLEDGEMENT

I understand my signature does not constitute agreement or disagreement. I acknowledge all required feedback was accomplished during the reporting period and upon receipt of this report.   ☐ Yes   ☐ No

SIGNATURE	DATE

PRIVACY ACT STATEMENT
AUTHORITY: Title 10, United States Code, Section 8013 and Executive Order 9397, 22 November 1943.
PURPOSE: Information is needed for verification of the individual's name and Social Security Number (SSN) as captured on the form at the time of the rating.
ROUTINE USES: May specifically be disclosed outside the DoD as a routine use pursuant to 5 U.S.C. 552a(b)(3).
DISCLOSURE: Disclosure is mandatory; SSN is used for positive identification.

AF FORM 911, 20080618   PREVIOUS EDITIONS ARE OBSOLETE   PRIVACY ACT INFORMATION: The information in this form is FOR OFFICIAL USE ONLY. Protect IAW the Privacy Act of 1974.

Appendix B. Interview Method and Analysis

As part of our data collection for this study, we conducted exploratory interviews with two senior enlisted leader advisory bodies, the EFDP, composed of chief master sergeants focused on effective development and utilization of the enlisted force, and the EBOD, composed of the MAJCOM chiefs and enlisted leaders serving in other strategic positions (25 chief master sergeants total). To include an officer perspective, we conducted interviews with a small sample of wing, group, and squadron commanders representative of different Air Force bases and mission types (16 officers total, ranging in rank from lieutenant colonel to major general).

Each interview lasted approximately 45–60 minutes. At least two RAND researchers conducted each interview, with one researcher leading the interview and the other taking verbatim notes. We used the same interview protocol for all participants; our questions focused primarily on the following three broad topics:

- master sergeant leadership duties
- master sergeant leadership knowledge, skills, abilities, and other characteristics to perform those duties
- perceptions of the effectiveness of the current promotion process.

We heard similar themes across all interviews and no longer heard new information toward the later sessions. Therefore, consistent with recommendations for qualitative research, the lack of new themes indicated we had reached theoretical saturation and additional interviews would not be necessary for our purposes.

Following recommendations for qualitative data analysis in the research literature (e.g., Corbin and Strauss, 2008; Miles and Huberman, 1994), we employed an iterative, multiphase approach in analyzing the interview data. We began by using an open-coding method to identify emerging themes that were relevant to the key research questions. In the second step of the analysis, we grouped these themes into more abstract categories to develop a coding scheme for the transcripts. Using the coding scheme, two research team members then hand-coded each interview transcript. To ensure sufficient interrater reliability in the coding, we calculated a statistic called *Cohen's kappa*, which indicated we had an acceptable level of interrater reliability across coding categories (0.70). For any disagreements that did exist, the coders met and discussed the differences until they reached agreement on the correct code that should be used in the final analysis. The majority of disagreements involved one coder having more codes in a thought unit (i.e., thought or statement provided in response to an interview question) than the other. Therefore, most disagreements were resolved by the addition of extra codes. Once all transcripts had been coded, we then employed a within-case and cross-case approach to identify

63

patterns in the data. This involved first examining each coded unit in the data separately to gain an in-depth understanding and then looking for similarities and differences across transcripts, particularly in terms of differences that may exist among the groups of participants in the study. The vast majority of answers were similar across SNCOs and officers. However, in the few places where we did notice substantial differences, we noted them in the results.

INTERVIEW PROTOCOL

INTRODUCTIONS, INFORMED CONSENT

Thank you very much for meeting with us today. We are here to gather information for a study sponsored by AF/A1D looking at the master sergeant promotion process.

<INSERT INFORMED CONSENT MATERIALS HERE>

We would like to start with some general background information about you.

GENERAL BACKGROUND

1. Please describe your current position (full title).
2. What are your main responsibilities?
3. How long have you served in this position?

MASTER SERGEANT LEADERSHIP RESPONSIBILITIES

4. Acknowledging differences in AFSCs, in general, what are the main duties/responsibilities of a master sergeant?
    a. What types of new duties will someone be given when promoted to a master sergeant?
5. What are the main leadership duties/responsibilities of a master sergeant?
6. Are there any job duties of a master sergeant that would be difficult to train/develop?
7. Have the duties of a master sergeant changed over the last five to ten years?
    a. If yes, how have they changed?
    b. How do you anticipate the job duties of a master sergeant might change over the next five to ten years?

MASTER SERGEANT LEADERSHIP KNOWLEDGE, SKILLS, ABILITIES, OR COMPETENCIES

We would now like to discuss the knowledge, skills, and abilities relevant to the duties/tasks you've identified. We'll begin by describing what we mean by those terms:

- *Knowledge: Organized body of information, such as facts, rules, and procedures. Examples: how to balance a budget, human resource policies.*
- *Skills: Developed capacities to perform tasks, predicated in part on the individual's possession of relevant underlying abilities. Skills include things like writing, reading comprehension, etc.*
- *Abilities: Usually refers to the cognitive or physical capabilities necessary to perform a job function. Examples include mathematical reasoning, oral expression, and strength.*

8. What knowledge, skills, and abilities do master sergeants need to be good leaders?
9. What characteristics do you believe distinguish a superior master sergeant from an average master sergeant?
10. Describe the characteristics of an ideal master sergeant.
11. Are there any gaps in the knowledge, skills, or abilities of current master sergeants?
    a. If yes, please describe the gaps.

12. Are you familiar with the current process for promotion to master sergeant?

13. How effective do you think the current promotion process is for selecting master sergeants (i.e., is it effective at selecting the right people)?

    a. What, if any, issues do you see with the current process?

    b. Do you think the right factors are being considered?

    c. Do you agree with the current distribution of points?

    d. What are positives of the current process?

14. What, if any, changes would you make to the current promotion process?

    a. Why?

15. How supportive do you feel others are of the current promotion process?

16. What challenges or barriers do you see in changing the current promotion process?

Appendix C. WAPS Factor Descriptive Statistics

This appendix provides an overview of descriptive statistics on the WAPS factors for promotion to master sergeant. Table C.1 shows the mean scores and standard deviation on each factor for all airmen eligible for promotion to master sergeant from promotion cycles 2000–2010. As discussed in the main body of the report, the mean EPR score, which accounts for the greatest number of WAPS points, is 134 out of 135 points, resulting in EPR scores having very little influence on promotion outcomes.

Table C.2 shows correlations between the different WAPS factors for airmen who were selected for promotion to master sergeant in promotion cycles 2000–2010. Overall, the correlations are small to medium in magnitude. In terms of the direction of the relationship, many of the correlations are negative. This may be expected, however, since the system operates as a compensatory model. For example, individuals who have higher TIG and TIS when they were promoted likely needed those points to compensate for lower test scores or EPR scores.

Table C.1. Score Distributions on WAPS Factors

WAPS Factor	Maximum Possible Points	Mean Score	Standard Deviation
SKT	100	54	12
PFE	100	55	12
TIS	40	35	5
TIG	60	27	7
Decorations	25	11	5
EPR	135	134	4

NOTE: Data from promotion cycles 2000–2010; N = 240,849; n = 210,807 for airmen with SKT scores.

Table C.2. Correlations Between WAPS Factors

	SKT	PFE	TIS	TIG	Decorative
PFE	0.26				
TIS	−0.44	−0.44			
TIG	−0.42	−0.51	0.58		
Decorations	−0.15	−0.17	0.13	0.07	
EPR	−0.02	−0.01	−0.15	−0.22	0.14

NOTE: Data from promotion cycles 2000–2010 for airmen selected for promotion to master sergeant; n = 57,495.

Appendix D. Overview of the Generalized Boosted Model

This appendix provides a brief overview of the GBM used to examine the relative influence of each WAPS factor on promotions (see Chapter Four). For readers interested in more technical details of GBM, we suggest consulting Ridgeway (2009) and references therein.

GBM is a flexible option for modeling dichotomous outcomes, such as promoted/not promoted. The standard GBM software calculates the "relative influence" of each explanatory variable on the outcome. Specifically, GBM models the probability of being promoted (versus not promoted) through piecewise constant combinations of the explanatory variables. The model is built iteratively, starting with a simple model, and gradually becoming more complex. For instance, the model may start by estimating that those who score below 90 on the SKT and who have a TIG score of less than 15 have a particular (low) probability of being promoted, whereas others have a somewhat higher probability of being promoted. At the next iteration, the model may give extra probability of being promoted to those who have a decorations score greater than 23, and so on.

The model makes thousands of such adjustments, each time adding or subtracting a constant value to the estimated probability of promotion for those whose test scores fall in an interval for one or two promotion factors. Although each step is a simple adjustment, the resulting model can be very complex.

With complicated models such as this one, overfitting the data is a concern. If we let the GBM algorithm run long enough, it is flexible enough that it would be able to fit the data perfectly. This would almost certainly result in poor predictive performance. GBM makes use of two techniques to avoid such overfitting. First, at each iteration, the adjustments to the probabilities are smaller than those that would optimize the fit. Thus, iteration-by-iteration, the changes to the probabilities are spread over the important variables. Secondly, GBM uses a method called cross-validation to choose an early stopping time in the algorithm, which results in a simpler model than if it were allowed to run until it achieves perfect fit. In the twofold cross-validation that we used, the dataset is randomly split into halves. The model is fit on each half and predicts the outcome in the other half. The number of iterations that achieves the best out-of-sample prediction is considered to be the correct level of complexity, and the reported model is fit on the entire dataset, but using the number of iterations (i.e., level of model complexity) suggested by the subdatasets.

After having fit the model with an appropriate level of model complexity, the GBM software produces a summary of the relative importance of each explanatory variable. The formula for its computation is given in Ridgeway (2009) and more details are available in Section 8.1 of Friedman (2001). In general, the software starts by tallying the improvement to the measure of fit that is attributable to an explanatory variable at each iteration in the algorithm. These improvements are then standardized so that the relative influences of each explanatory variable are on a scale between 0 and 100 percent, and sum to one.

Appendix E. Research Findings on Evaluation Criteria for Each Assessment Method

Using information provided in quantitative reviews (i.e., meta-analyses) that aggregate results from multiple studies, Table E.1 presents an overview of the primary assessment methods and their strengths and weakness. The validity for each assessment is presented first as the most important criterion for evaluation. The remaining criteria (i.e., candidate acceptance, cost, diversity fairness) are all important to Air Force objectives, but are presented in no particular order, given that they represent different trade-offs to be weighed.

Each quantitative review examined the relationship between a specific measure or construct (e.g., job knowledge) and a specific outcome or criteria (e.g., overall job performance). The validity estimates provided in the second column represent the population effect sizes, which indicate the strength and direction of the relationship between measures and criteria. These effect sizes can vary from –1.00 to 1.00, with the positive or negative sign indicating the direction of the relationship while the distance from zero indicates the strength of the relationship. For example, an effect size of 0.50 between job knowledge and performance indicates a strong positive relationship, such that performance improves as one's knowledge increases. A slightly different interpretation can be made for the last column, which examines diversity fairness. The d-values indicate the difference between how one group (e.g., Black) and another group (e.g., White) scores on a particular measure. A d-value of zero indicates no difference between the two groups; a d-value of 1.00 (i.e., one-standard deviation difference) indicates a large difference. In cases of large or very large differences, the d-values will exceed 1.00. In some cases, the d-values provided are tentative, which suggests that more research is needed to increase our understanding of the conditions under which group differences vary. For example, research suggests that biodata measures have a d-value of 0.39; however, the true difference between groups may vary depending on which constructs are measured in the biodata measure (Bobko and Roth, 2013). Finally, it is important to note that diversity fairness has several definitions and a significant difference between groups by itself should not determine its use. Although a full discussion of diversity fairness is beyond the scope of this report, other factors—such as differential prediction or the extent to which an assessment is a better predictor of job performance for one subgroup compared to another—should be fully evaluated.

In addition to evaluating the fairness and validity of each selection method, we also evaluated candidate acceptance (fourth column) and relative cost (fifth column). The relative acceptance of each method was categorized into low, moderate, or high based on meta-analyses examining applicant reactions to different selection methods. However, it is important to note that since our review focused on assessments that were supported by research and could be linked to job requirements, assessments that have low acceptance (e.g., personal contacts such as relatives and friends) were not included.

Finally, the relative cost of each method was categorized as low, moderate, and high based on our estimates of resources, time, and personnel required to develop, administer, score, and interpret each method. Similar to other cost analyses of personnel selection measures,[1] our estimates of costs are made in relative terms to other assessments and included a broad evaluation of development costs as well as implementation costs. Among the development costs we considered were the technical expertise and time required to construct and validate a new assessment. Implementation costs included resources required to administer (personnel, equipment, facilities) and score an assessment (technical expertise, information technology). In addition to providing the relative costs of a promotion board, the actual costs were estimated using historical information provided by the Air Force. Although actual costs cannot be provided for the other assessments, our analysis of the relative costs of a promotion board suggest that it would cost more than self-report assessments (e.g., personality, biodata) but less than assessments requiring interaction with promotion candidates (e.g., assessment centers, structured interviews).

To help interpret the data for each column in Table E.1, we provide an explanation of the evaluation criteria for SJTs. Beginning in the second column, there are three different estimates or ranges of estimates provided for the validity of an SJT, indicating different constructs measured by an SJT. That is, the meta-analyses included SJTs designed to measure the ability to lead, supervise, and work in a team. In general, the approximate estimates range between 0.3 and 0.4, suggesting a moderate positive relationship between how individuals score on SJTs and how they perform in their jobs.

The third column indicates the criteria used in the validity studies. Although we only included studies using job performance as the criteria, other studies could have used different criteria, such as training performance. The fourth column indicates that candidates would be expected to have moderate to favorable reactions toward an SJT. More favorable reactions would be expected to the extent that items and responses on the SJT represent actual and specific versus hypothetical situations encountered by master sergeants. The fifth column indicates that SJTs are relatively inexpensive compared to other assessments. Although a customized SJT requires time and technical expertise to develop, the assessment can be administered and scored by computer, which significantly decreases long-term costs.

Finally, the last column shows the diversity fairness of each assessment. As indicated above, the *d*-values represent the magnitude of the difference between groups. Different estimates are provided to show how the difference between groups on an SJT can vary by the construct measured.

---

[1] Our cost analyses are consistent with guidance provided by the Occupational Information Network website (undated) and the Office of Personnel Management's *Assessment Decision Guide* (undated).

Table E.1. Research Findings on Evaluation Criteria for Various Assessment Methods

Selection Method	Validity	Criteria	Candidate Acceptance	Relative Cost	Diversity Fairness (d values)
	Neuroticism (opposite of emotional stability) (−0.17)[a] Extraversion (0.24) Openness (0.15) Agreeableness (0.14) Conscientiousness (0.13)	Observer ratings Transformational leadership (e.g., subordinates, peers)			d = 0.09[b]
	Multiple R (0.23 to 0.27)[c]	Objective and overall individual job performance			**Black-White**[d] Emotional stability (−0.09) Extraversion (−0.16) Openness (−0.10) Agreeableness (−0.03); Conscientiousness (0.07)
Personality	Multiple R (.037)[c]	Individual teamwork	Moderate	Low	**Asian-White**[d] Emotional stability (−0.12) Extraversion (−0.14) Openness (0.11) Agreeableness (0.63) Conscientiousness (0.11)
	Multiple R (0.45)[c]	Avoiding organizational deviance			**Hispanic-White**[d] Emotional stability (0.03) Extraversion (−0.02) Openness (−0.02) Agreeableness (−0.05) Conscientiousness (0.08)
	Conscientiousness (0.31)[e]	Job performance			
Biodata	Uncorrected (0.28)[f] Corrected (0.35)[e]	Job performance	Moderate	Low to moderate	Tentative average (0.39)[b]

73

Selection Method	Validity	Criteria	Candidate Acceptance	Relative Cost	Diversity Fairness (d values)
Structured Interview	(0.44)[g] (0.51)[e] Job knowledge/skills (0.33)[h] Conscientiousness (0.37) Interpersonal skills (0.40) Leadership (0.40) Organizational fit (values and moral standards) (0.58)	Job performance Job performance Job performance evaluations	High	High	(0.31 to 0.46)[b]
Work Sample	(0.33)[i]	Job performance	High	Moderate to high	Overall (0.73) Oral communication (0.27) Leadership/persuasion (0.27) Written skills (0.70) Cognitive processes and job knowledge (0.80)[b]
	Multiple R (0.40)[j] **Dimensions** Organizing/planning (0.35) Problem solving (0.32) Influencing others (0.31) Communication (0.27) Consideration of others (0.24)	Job performance			
Assessment Center	Composite (0.36)[k] **Dimensions** Problem solving (.39) Influencing others (.38) Organizing/planning (.37) Consideration of others (.35) Drive (.31) Communication (.33) (0.37)[e]	Job performance Job performance	High	High	(0.56)[b]
Situational Judgment Test	Supervisory (.21 to .41)[l] Leadership construct (.28)[f] Teamwork skills (.38)	Job performance Job performance	Moderate to high	Low to moderate	Weighted average (0.38) Interpersonal (0.19) Cognitive and job knowledge (0.65) Leadership (1.02)[b]

Selection Method	Validity	Criteria	Candidate Acceptance	Relative Cost	Diversity Fairness (*d* values)
Board Ratings	Unknown		Moderate	Moderate to high	Unknown

NOTE: The Multiple R represents the correlation coefficient for a set of Big Five personality factors and the specified criterion.

SOURCES:

[a] Bono and Judge (2004, pp. 901–910)

[b] Bobko and Roth (2013)

[c] Ones, Dilchert, et al. (2007, pp. 995–1027)

[d] Foldes, Duehr, and Ones (2008, pp. 579–616)

[e] Schmidt and Hunter (1998, pp. 262–274)

[f] Christian, M. S., B. D. Edwards, and J. C. Bradley, "Situational Judgment Tests: Constructs Assessed and a Meta-Analysis of Their Criterion-Related Validities," *Personnel Psychology*, Vol. 63, 2010, pp. 83-117.

[g] McDaniel, Whetzel, et al. (1994, pp. 599–616)

[h] Huffcutt, Conway, et al. (2001, pp. 897–913)

[i] Roth, Bobko, et al. (2008, pp. 637–661)

[j] Meriac et al. (2008, pp. 1042–1052)

[k] Arthur et al. (2003, pp. 125–154)

[l] McDaniel, Morgeson et al. (2001, pp. 730–740)

Appendix F. Estimated Cost of a Master Sergeant Promotion Board

In this appendix, we present details on our estimate for the annual cost of a board for promotion to master sergeant. Costs used in this analysis included (1) the opportunity cost of board members being removed from their primary duty, (2) costs to convene the board, (3) and administrative costs. In the following sections, we describe the various costs that need to be considered and our estimate of the costs of a senior master sergeant board as a baseline for master sergeant board costs. We then examine the cost of master sergeant promotion boards under four scenarios, based on possible board composition and the number of eligible records reviewed:

- **Option 1:** All eligible records are reviewed and scored by the board and the staffing levels are similar to those used for senior master sergeant promotion boards.
- **Option 2:** All eligible records are reviewed and scored by the board while the boards are staffed with members lower in rank than the senior master sergeant boards.
- **Option 3:** The board reviews and scores some portion of the eligible records and the staffing levels are similar to those used for senior master sergeant promotion boards.
- **Option 4:** The board reviews and scores some portion of the eligible records while the boards are staffed with members lower in rank than the senior master sergeant boards.

Promotion Board Costs

In this section, we describe the costs associated with the senior master sergeant promotion boards based on information from the Air Force Personnel Center, USAF Selection Board Secretariat, and public Department of Defense sources. This provides a baseline with which to estimate the costs of a master sergeant promotion board.

Opportunity Cost of Board Duty

To estimate the cost of operating senior master sergeant boards, we first examined the opportunity cost of taking members away from their primary duty, expressed as days away by grade. Currently, senior master sergeant boards review approximately 13,000 eligible records each year. The process, conducted annually, takes approximately three weeks, beginning with two days of training for the board members. The board is composed of 14 panels chaired by a brigadier general. Each panel is staffed with one colonel and two chief master sergeants. In addition, the board requires support from seven senior master sergeant administrative assistants. Table F.1 provides a summary of the opportunity cost (days absent) by grade.

Table F.1. Opportunity Costs for Board Members

Grade	Days
Brigadier general	15
Colonel	210
Chief master sergeant	420
Senior master sergeant	105

It is important to note that the relative value of these days is difficult to determine. For example, to what extent does a brigadier general wing commander's absence impact the completion of his or her duties and the wing's operation, as compared to a senior master sergeant section chief's absence from a wing? One might wish to use the member's compensation as a method for valuing the opportunity cost at each grade. However, the extent to which compensation accurately reflects impact on productivity with the absence of each grade is unclear. Therefore, we felt that the number of days required by each grade provided a better picture of opportunity costs.

Travel and Per Diem

Promotion boards are held at Randolph Air Force Base, so travel and per diem costs must be considered. We assume that all senior master sergeant board members, including the administrative assistants, will incur travel, transportation, and per diem costs. Per diem costs include three separate components: lodging, meals, and incidentals (M&IE). The maximum lodging rate for San Antonio at the time of the study (fiscal year 2012) was $106, and the M&IE rate was $66. Therefore, the daily per diem cost for each eligible staff member was $172. On travel days, M&IE rates are reimbursed at 75 percent, so total per diem for travel days was $155.50.

As mentioned, the board proceedings for senior master sergeant promotions generally take three weeks. In addition to the 15 days that board members are actively working, per diem must be included for the two weekends they will need to stay at Randolph Air Force Base, as well as two travel days. Therefore, for each eligible staff member on the senior master sergeant promotion board, we estimate total per diem costs to be roughly $3,580.

For travel, we assume that all eligible staff will be traveling by plane. However, we do not have historical data on the locations from which various senior master sergeant board participants typically travel. Instead we used an average of costs from five cities across the United States that are likely origins of travel and represent a range of distances from San Antonio. Specifically, we used flight costs for Washington, D.C.; Dayton, Ohio; St. Louis, Mo; Norfolk, Va.; and Colorado Springs, Colo.; to compute an average expected flight cost. The federal government obtains low-cost, flexible tickets through the City Pairs Program (see Table F.2 for one-way flight costs). Based on the ticket prices listed for the City Pairs Program for our five representative locations, the average round-trip flight cost per person is estimated to be approximately $373. In addition, the average government rate for a rental car in the San Antonio area for the three-week board period is $477, for a total travel cost of approximately $850 per member.

The total cost for travel, transportation, and per diem for a senior master sergeant promotion board is estimated to be roughly $221,500 (see Table F.2).

Table F.2. Total Cost for E-8 Board Membership (14 Panels, 15 Working Days)

	Senior Master Sergeant	Chief Master Sergeant	Colonel	Brigadier General
Number of board members	7	28	14	1
Travel/transportation per member	$850	$850	$850	$850
Per diem per member	$3,580	$3,580	$3,580	$3,580
Total cost per member	$4,430	$4,430	$4,430	$4,430
Total cost at each grade	$31,010	$124,040	$62,020	$4,430

Records Upkeep

There are also costs associated with maintaining and preparing records for the board members to review and score. At the time of this research, AFPC's Board Secretariat employed 27 people at a cost of $2.1 million to maintain officer and enlisted records. This equates to an average cost per employee of $77,778. They estimate nine full-time-equivalents (FTEs) are required to prepare the records—which number more than 15,000—that enlisted boards review each year. Given the number of records going before senior master sergeant and chief master sergeant boards, this means it currently takes approximately one FTE ($77,778) to maintain 1,686 enlisted records.

Estimated Cost for a Master Sergeant Promotion Board

Using the above senior master sergeant promotion board costs as a baseline, this section describes the range of costs that might be expected for a master sergeant promotion board by looking at four options for promotion board implementation.

Differences Between Senior Master Sergeant and Master Sergeant Promotion Boards

The primary difference between master sergeant and senior master sergeant boards is the number of eligible records. There are approximately 60 percent more eligible master sergeant records in a given year, or approximately 21,000 annually. This increased caseload requires increases in the number of panels, the length of the board process, or both (relative to what is currently used for senior master sergeant boards). We estimate (based on the average number of records reviewed and the average length of the boards for fiscal years 2009–2012) that each eligible senior master sergeant record takes an average of 6.7 minutes per panel to review. It is not clear whether it would take a similar amount of time, on average, to review a master sergeant record, so we assume a similar per-record time requirement. The exact assumptions regarding the number of panels needed are discussed in the next section.

Estimated Costs for a Master Sergeant Promotion Board—Four Options

Table F.3 presents the required board member composition for four alternate master sergeant promotion board options:

- **Option 1:** Board reviews/scores all eligible records with board staffing levels similar to senior master sergeant promotion boards.
- **Option 2:** Board reviews/scores all eligible records with boards staffed by members with lower rank than senior master sergeant boards.
- **Option 3:** Board reviews/scores 50 percent of the eligible records with board staffing levels that are similar to senior master sergeant promotion boards.
- **Option 4:** Board reviews/scores 50 percent of the eligible records with boards staffed by members with lower rank than senior master sergeant boards.

The variations across the options occur in the number of records reviewed, the number of panels, and the rank of the board members. The E-8 staff requirements are included in the first row of the table as a source of comparison. For each of the master sergeant board options, master sergeants serve as administrative assistants.

Table F.3. Staffing Needs for Promotion Board Options

Board	Option	Records	Panels	E-7 Administrative Assistants	E-8 Administrative Assistants	E-8s	E-9s	0-5s	0-6s	0-7s
E-8	Comparison	13K	14		7		28		14	1
E-7	Option 1	21K	22	11			44		22	1
E-7	Option 2	21K	22	11		44		22	1	
E-7	Option 3	10.5K	14	7			28		14	1
E-7	Option 4	10.5K	14	7		28		14	1	

Options 1 and 2 are generated under the assumption that all eligible records will be reviewed. As previously noted, to account for this near doubling of records, the board would need to either increase the number of panels or increase the length of time the board meets. While the costs will be nearly identical regardless of which option is chosen to meet staffing needs, we suspect that it would be difficult to expect board members to commit more than three weeks of time away from their home station assignment, so we assume that the time commitment would remain fixed at three weeks and that additional panels would be staffed. If the senior master sergeant board time of three weeks is maintained and we assume that it will take approximately the same amount of

80

time on average to review a master sergeant record (approximately 6½ minutes per record), then we estimate that 22 panels would be needed. Option 1 assumes an identical staffing ratio to that currently used for the senior master sergeant promotion board, with each panel staffed by one colonel and two chief master sergeants, and a brigadier general chairing the board. Option 2 presents an alternative staffing model, in which both enlisted and officer board positions are staffed with members of the next lower rank.

Options 3 and 4 represent a substantive difference in the way master sergeant boards are conducted relative to senior master sergeant boards. Under these options, only half of all eligible records would be reviewed. This scenario is intended to represent a situation in which a hurdle selection system is utilized to reduce the total number of records reviewed by the board. A hurdle system occurs when candidates who do not exceed a minimum score on an initial evaluation are excluded from further consideration. For example, other WAPS scores (PFE, SKT, EPR, decorations, TIS, and TIG) could be used to rank-order promotion eligible individuals within each AFSC. Then, only the records for the top 50 percent from each rank-ordered list would be sent to a board for scoring. For the purposes of this study, we assume that the initial hurdle (e.g., ranking by other WAPS scores) would bring no additional costs. The impact on the overall cost would be driven only by changes in the size of the board. Because the initial hurdle already narrows the group seen by the board to those most competitive for promotion, meaning those likely to be easily dismissed will already be removed, we assume that the review time per record may be somewhat higher and provide an additional two minutes (totaling 8½ minutes[1]) for the top 50 percent of eligible records. Similar to the first two options, Option 3 assumes an identical staffing ratio to that currently used for the senior master sergeant promotion board, with each panel staffed by one colonel and two chief master sergeants, and a brigadier general chairing the board. Option 4 presents an alternative staffing model, in which both enlisted and officer board positions are staffed with members of the next lower rank.

Based on the estimated staffing needs, the opportunity cost expressed in total days away from primary duty by grade for the senior master sergeant board and the four proposed options for master sergeant boards are presented in Table F.4.

---

[1] This is a modest increase and more time may actually be needed in practice. As stated, we estimate that the average time per person per record at the E-8 board is 6 minutes, 46 seconds. We estimate the average time per record per person for the E-9 board is 23 minutes, 51 seconds. We would not expect the competition at an E-7 board to be nearly as steep as at an E-9 board—only 1 percent of the enlisted force at any time holds the grade of chief master sergeant and only 3 percent can hold the top two grades, senior master sergeant and chief master sergeant.

Table F.4. Days Away from Primary Duty—Totals for Promotion Board Options

Board	Option	Master Sergeant Administrative Assistants	Senior Master Sergeant Administrative Assistants	Senior Master Sergeant	Chief Master Sergeant	Lieutenant Colonels	Colonels	Brigadier Generals
E-8	Comparison		105		420		210	15
E-7	Option 1	165			660		330	15
E-7	Option 2	165		660		330	15	
E-7	Option 3	105			420		210	15
E-7	Option 4	105		420		210	15	

In terms of monetary costs, there will again be costs for travel and per diem and records maintenance and preparation. Travel and per diem costs can be calculated using the same figures as for senior master sergeant boards, but with the adjustment in staffing for each option. For records maintenance and preparation, as previously stated, it takes approximately 1 FTE at a cost of roughly $78,000 to maintain 1,686 records. For Options 1 and 2, where all records would be reviewed, we can estimate an additional 12.5 FTE for an estimated annual cost of $975,000. For Options 3 and 4, we estimate 6.5 FTE for $507,000. Table F.5 shows the total estimated costs for travel, transportation, per diem and records maintenance for these options.

Table F.5. Estimated Costs for Promotion Board Options

Board	Option	Travel/ Transportation	Per Diem	Records Maintenance	Total Cost
E-8	Comparison	$42,500	$179,000	$600,600	$822,100
E-7	Option 1	$66,300	$279,240	$975,000	$1,320,540
E-7	Option 2	$66,300	$279,240	$975,000	$1,320,540
E-7	Option 3	$42,500	$179,000	$507,000	$728,500
E-7	Option 4	$42,500	$179,000	$507,000	$728,500

Examining Tables F.4 and F.5 together, the benefit of Option 2 is the reduced grade for the number of days away—a reduced opportunity cost. For Option 3, the monetary costs for the board are reduced by half, and the total number of days away for board members are also reduced. For Option 4, the monetary costs are reduced as well as the number of days away for board members, including a reduction in the grade of board members, or a reduced opportunity cost. Overall, procedures and policies that reduce the number of records to be reviewed appear to provide more savings, both monetary and opportunity costs (days away), than just reducing the rank of the board members alone. The Air Force will need to determine whether having a reduction in the grade of board members, as reflected in Option 4, provides an additional benefit they should pursue as well.

Changes Due to the Electronic Board Operations Support System

In estimating board costs, it is important to note that AFPC recently implemented the eBoss, for active-duty SNCO evaluation boards in 2013. Our research was completed prior to implementation—but, if implemented as planned, this electronic system is expected to reduce the staff and time needed to maintain and prepare records for board consideration. Because eBoss takes advantage of records available in ARMS, the 27 personnel who currently maintain the records will no longer be needed to the same degree, eliminating most of this personnel cost. In addition, administrative assistants will no longer be required. As shown in Table F.6, this significantly reduces the financial cost of holding promotion boards.

Table F.6. Estimated Costs for Promotion Board Options (Travel, Transportation, Per Diem, Records Maintenance)

Board	Option	Current Paper Records Total Cost	eBOSS Total Cost
E-7	Option 1	$1,320,540	$314,530
E-7	Option 2	$1,320,540	$314,530
E-7	Option 3	$728,500	$190,490
E-7	Option 4	$728,500	$190,490

However, at the time of this research, AFPC staff did not expect eBoss to reduce the time it takes for board members to review records. Therefore, the opportunity cost in board members' days away from their primary assignment remains the same as in the current paper-based system.

Summary

Overall, procedures and policies that reduce the number of records to be reviewed appear to provide more savings in both monetary and opportunity costs, in terms of days away, than just reducing the rank of the board members alone. The establishment of eBoss also significantly reduces the monetary costs of holding a master sergeant board under all options. However, it is important to consider that any changes in policy may also add costs beyond just holding a board. For example, if it is determined that all eligible master sergeants will need a senior rater review, additional processing will be required for nearly 21,000 EPRs distributed across the Air Force. Again, these costs are difficult to quantify; however, even a small change can result in a significant workload based on the large number of eligible airmen.

References

Anderson, N., J. F. Salgado, and U. R. Hulsheger, "Applicant Reactions in Selection: Comprehensive Meta-Analysis into Reaction Generalization Versus Situational Specificity," *International Journal of Selection and Assessment*, Vol. 18, 2010, pp. 291–304.

Arthur, W., E. A. Day, T. L. McNelly, and P. S. Edens, "A Meta-Analysis of the Criterion-Related Validity of Assessment Center Dimensions," *Personnel Psychology*, Vol. 56, 2003, pp. 125–154.

Arvey, R. D., and K. R. Murphy, "Performance Evaluation in Work Settings," *Annual Review of Psychology*, Vol. 49, 1998, pp. 141–168.

Avolio, B. J., J. J. Sosik, D. I. Jung, and Y. Berson, "Leadership Models, Methods, and Applications, " in W. Borman, D. Ilgen, and R. Komoski eds., *Handbook of Psychology, Vol. 12—Industrial and Organizational Psychology*, New York: Wiley, 2003, pp. 277–307.

Barrick, M. R., and M. K. Mount, "The Big 5 Personality Dimensions and Job-Performance—A Metaanalysis," *Personnel Psychology*, Vol. 44, No. 1, 1991, pp. 1–26.

Bass, B. and R. Bass, *The Bass Handbook of Leadership: Theory, Research, and Managerial Applications,* New York: Free Press, 2008.

Bobko, P., and P. L. Roth, "Reviewing, Categorizing, and Analyzing, the Literature on Black-White Mean Differences for Predictors of Job Performance: Verifying Some Perceptions and Updating/Correcting Others," *Personnel Psychology*, 2013, pp. 91–126.

Bobko, P., P. L. Roth, and D. Potosky, "Derivation and Implications of a Meta-Analytic Matrix Incorporating Cognitive Ability, Alternative Predictors, and Job Performance," *Personnel Psychology*, Vol. 52, No. 3, 1999, pp. 561–589.

Bono, J. E., and T. A. Judge, "Personality and Transformational and Transactional Leadership: A Meta-Analysis," *Journal of Applied Psychology*, Vol. 89, No. 5, 2004, pp. 901–910.

Borman, W. C., E. D. Pulakos, L. A. White, and S. H. Oppler, "Models of Supervisory Job-Performance Ratings," *Journal of Applied Psychology*, Vol. 76, No. 6, 1991, pp. 863-872.

Borman, W. C., M. A. Hanson, S. H. Oppler, E. D. Pulakos, and L. A. White, "Role of Early Supervisory Experience in Supervisor Performance," *Journal of Applied Psychology*, Vol. 78, No. 3, 1993, pp. 443–449.

Borman, W. C., L. A. White, and D. W. Dorsey, "Effects of Ratee Task-Performance and Interpersonal Factors on Supervisor and Peer Performance Ratings," *Journal of Applied Psychology*, Vol. 80, No. 1, 1995, pp. 168–177.

Bowler, M. C., and D. J. Woehr, "A Meta-Analytic Evaluation of the Impact of Dimension and Exercise Factors on Assessment Center Ratings," *Journal of Applied Psychology*, Vol. 91, 2006, pp. 1114–1124.

Brannick, M. T., E. L. Levine, and F. P. Morgeson, *Job and Work Analysis: Methods, Research, and Applications for Human Resource Management*, Thousand Oaks, Calif.: Sage Publications, 2007.

Callinan, M., and I. T. Robertson, "Work Sample Testing," *International Journal of Selection and Assessment*, Vol. 8, 2000, pp. 248–260.

Campbell, J. P. and D. J. Knapp, eds., *Exploring the Limits in Personnel Selection and Classification*, Mahwah, N.J.: Lawrence Erlbaum Associates, 2001.

Catano, V. M., W. Darr, and C. A. Campbell, "Performance Appraisal of Behavior-Based Competencies: A Reliable and Valid Procedure," *Personnel Psychology*, Vol. 60, 2007, pp. 201–230.

Chan, K. Y. and F. Drasgow, "Toward a Theory of Individual Differences and Leadership: Understanding the Motivation to Lead," *Journal of Applied Psychology*, Vol. 86, No. 3, 2001, pp. 481–498.

Chiaburu, D. S., I. S. Oh, C. M. Berry, N. Li, and R. G. Gardner, "The Five-Factor Model of Personality Traits and Organizational Citizenship Behaviors: A Meta-Analysis," *Journal of Applied Psychology*, Vol., 96, No. 6, 2011, pp. 1140–1166.

Christian, M. S., B. D. Edwards, and J. C. Bradley, "Situational Judgment Tests: Constructs Assessed and a Meta-Analysis of Their Criterion-Related Validities," *Personnel Psychology*, Vol. 63, 2010, pp. 83–117.

Connelly, M. S., J. A. Gilbert, S. J. Zaccaro, K. V. Threlfall, M. A. Marks, and M. D. Mumford, "Exploring the Relationship of Leadership Skills and Knowledge to Leader Performance," *Leadership Quarterly*, Vol. 11, No. 1, 2000, pp. 65–86.

Corbin, Juliet M., and Anselm L. Strauss, *Basics of Qualitative Research: Techniques and Procedures for Developing Grounded Theory*, 3rd ed., Thousand Oaks, Calif.: Sage Publications, 2008.

Dye, D. A., M. Reck, and M. A. McDaniel, "The Validity of Job Knowledge Measures," *International Journal of Selection and Assessment*, Vol. 1, 1993, pp. 153-157.

EEOC—*See* Equal Employment Opportunity Commission.

Equal Employment Opportunity Commission, Civil Service Commission, Department of Labor, and Department of Justice, "Uniform Guidelines on Employee Selection Procedures," *Federal Register*, 43, 38290–39315, 1978.

Foldes, H. J., E. E. Duehr, and D. S. Ones, "Group Differences in Personality: Meta-Analyses Comparing Five U.S. Racial Groups," *Personnel Psychology*, Vol. 61, No. 3, 2008, pp. 579–616.

Ford, L. A., R. C. Campbell, J. P. Campbell, D. J. Knapp, and C. B. Walker, *21st Century Soldiers and Noncommissioned Officers: Critical Predictors of Performance*, Technical Report 1102, U.S. Army Research Institute for the Behavioral and Social Sciences, May 2000.

Freidman, J. H., "Greedy Function Approximation: A Gradient Boosting Matching," *Annals of Statistics*, Vol. 29, No. 5, 2001, pp. 1189–1232.

Goldberg, L. R., "An Alternative Description of Personality—The Big-5 Factor Structure," *Journal of Personality and Social Psychology*, Vol. 59, No. 6, 1990, pp. 1216–1229.

Goldberg, L. R., "The Structure of Phenotypic Personality Traits," *American Psychologist*, Vol. 48, No. 1, 1993, pp. 26–34.

Hall, Francis J., and Clark K. Nelsen, *A Historical Perspective of the United States Air Force Enlisted Personnel Promotion Policy (1947-1980)*, Master's thesis, Wright-Patterson Air Force Base, Ohio: Air Force Institute of Technology, LSSR-53-80, June 1980. As of February 25, 2013:
http://www.dtic.mil/cgi-bin/GetTRDoc?Location=U2&doc=GetTRDoc.pdf&AD=ADA088777

Harold, C. M., L. A. McFarland, and J. A. Weekley, "The Validity of Verifiable and Nonverifiable Biodata Items: An Examination Across Applicants and Incumbents," *International Journal of Selection and Assessment*, Vol. 14, 2006, pp. 336–346.

Hoffman, B., D. Woehr, R. Maldagen-Youngjohn, and B. Lyons, "Great Man or Great Myth? A Quantitative Review of the Relationship Between Individual Differences and Leader Effectiveness," *Journal of Occupational and Organizational Psychology*, Vol. 84, 2011, pp. 347–381.

Hogan, J., P. Barrett, and R. Hogan, "Personality Measurement, Faking, and Employment Selection," *Journal of Applied Psychology*, Vol. 92, 2007, pp. 1270–1285.

Hogan, R., J. Hogan, and B. W. Roberts, "Personality Measurement and Employment Decisions—Questions and Answers," *American Psychologist*, Vol. 51, No. 5, 1996, pp. 469–477.

Howard, A., "An Assessment of Assessment Centers," *Academy of Management Journal*, Vol. 17, 1974, pp. 115–134.

Huffcutt, A. I., J. M. Conway, P. L. Roth, and N. J. Stone, "Identification and Meta-Analytic Assessment of Psychological Constructs Measured in Employment Interviews," *Journal of Applied Psychology*, Vol. 85, No. 5, 2001, pp. 897–913.

Huffcutt, A. I., and D. J. Woehr, "Further Analysis of Employment Interview Validity: A Quantitative Evaluation of Interviewer-Related Structuring Methods," *Journal of Organizational Behavior*, Vol. 20, 1999, pp. 549–560.

Ingerick, M., K. L. Schwartz, and J. J. Weismuller, *Identifying Leader Talent: Alternative Predictors for U.S. Air Force Junior Officer Selection and Assessment*, AFCAPS-FR-2010-0020, Air Force Personnel Center Strategic Research and Assessment, Randolph Air Force Base, Texas, November 2006.

Judge, T. A., J. E. Bono, R. Ilies, M. W. Gerhardt, "Personality and Leadership: A Qualitative and Quantitative Review," *Journal of Applied Psychology*, Vol. 87, No. 4, 2002, pp. 765-780.

Judge, T. A., A. E. Colbert, and R. Ilies, "Intelligence and Leadership: A Quantitative Review and Test of Theoretical Propositions," *Journal of Applied Psychology*, Vol. 89, No. 3, 2004, pp. 542–552.

Judge, T. A., and R. F. Piccolo, "Transformational and Transactional Leadership: A Meta-analytic Test of their Relative Validity," *Journal of Applied Psychology,* Vol. 89, 2004, pp. 755–768.

Knapp, D. J., J. L. Burnfield, C. E. Sager, G. W. Waugh, J. P Campbell, C. L. Reeve, R. C. Campbell, L. A. White, and T. S. Heffner, *Development of Predictor and Criterion Measures for the NCO21 Research Program*, Technical Report 1128, U.S. Army Research Institute for the Behavioral and Social Sciences, June 2002.

Koplyay, J. B., *Field Test of the Weighted Airman Promotion System: Phase I. Analysis of the Promotion Board Component in the Weighted Factors System*, Lackland Air Force Base, Texas: Air Force Human Resources Laboratory, AFHRL-TR-69-10, April 1969.

Kozlowski, Steve W., Georgia T. Chao, and Robert F. Morrison, "Games Raters Play: Politics, Strategies, and Impression Management in Performance Appraisal," in J. Smither, ed., *Performance Appraisal: State of the Art in Practice*, San Francisco, Calif.: Jossey-Bass, 1998, pp. 163–208.

Krajewski, H. T., R. D. Goffin, J. M. McCarthy, M. G. Rothstein, and N. Johnston, "Comparing the Validity of Structured Interviews for Managerial-Level Employees: Should We Look to the Past or Focus on the Future?" *Journal of Occupational and Organizational Psychology*, Vol. 79, 2006, pp. 411–432.

Lawler, E. E., "The Folly of Forced Ranking," *Strategy + Business*, Vol. 28, 2002, pp. 28–32.

Lefkowitz, J., M. I. Gebbia, T. Balsam, and L. Dunn, "Dimensions of Biodata Items and Their Relationships to Item Validity," *Journal of Occupational and Organizational Psychology*, Vol. 72, 1999, pp. 331–350.

Macan, T. H., M. J. Avedon, M. Paese, and D. E. Smith, "The Effects of Applicants Reactions to Cognitive-Ability Tests and an Assessment-Center," *Personnel Psychology*, Vol. 47, 1994, pp. 715-738.

McCloy, R. A., J. P. Campbell, and R. Cudeck, "A Confirmatory Test of a Model of Performance Determinants," *Journal of Applied Psychology*, Vol. 79, 1994, pp. 493-505.

McDaniel, M. A., N. S. Hartman, D. L. Whetzel, and W. L. Grubb, "Situational Judgment Tests, Response Instructions, and Validity: A Meta-Analysis," *Personnel Psychology*, Vol. 60, 2007, pp. 63–91.

McDaniel, M. A., F. P. Morgeson, E. B. Finnegan, M. A. Campion, and E. P. Braverman, "Use of Situational Judgment Tests to Predict Job Performance: A Clarification of the Literature," *Journal of Applied Psychology*, Vol. 86, 2001, pp. 730–740.

McDaniel, M. A., F. L. Schmidt, and J. E. Hunter, "Job Experience Correlates of Job-Performance," *Journal of Applied Psychology*, Vol. 73, No. 2, 1988, pp. 327–330.

McDaniel, M. A., D. L. Whetzel, F. L. Schmidt, and S. D. Maurer, "The Validity of Employment Interviews: A Comprehensive Review and Meta-Analysis," *Journal of Applied Psychology*, Vol. 79, 1994, pp. 599–616.

McEnrue, M. P., "Length of Experience and the Performance of Managers in the Establishment Phase of Their Careers," *Academy of Management Journal*, Vol. 31, No. 1, 1988, pp. 175–185.

Meriac, J. P., B. J. Hoffman, D. J. Woehr, and M. S. Fleisher, "Further Evidence for the Validity of Assessment Center Dimensions: A Meta-Analysis of the Incremental Criterion-Related Validity of Dimension Ratings," *Journal of Applied Psychology*, Vol. 93, 2008, pp. 1042–1052.

Mero, N. P., and S. J. Motowidlo, "Effects of Rater Accountability on the Accuracy and the Favorability of Performance Ratings," *Journal of Applied Psychology*, Vol. 80, No. 4, 1995, pp. 517–524.

Mero, N. P., S. J. Motowidlo, and A. L. Anna, "Effects of Accountability on Rating Behavior and Rater Accuracy," *Journal of Applied Social Psychology*, Vol. 33, No. 12, 2003, pp. 2493–2514.

Miles, Mathew B., and A. Michael Huberman, *Qualitative Data Analysis: An Expanded Sourcebook*, 2nd ed., Thousand Oaks, Calif.: Sage Publications, 1994.

Motowidlo, S. J., M. D. Dunnette, and G. W. Carter, "An Alternative Selection Procedure: The Low-Fidelity Simulation," *Journal of Applied Psychology*, Vol. 75, 1990, pp. 640–647.

Motowidlo, S. J., and N. Tippins, "Further Studies of the Low-Fidelity Simulation in the Form of a Situational Inventory," *Journal of Occupational and Organizational Psychology*, Vol. 66, 1993, pp. 337–344.

Mueller-Hanson, R., E. D. Heggestad, and G. C. Thornton, "Faking and Selection: Considering the Use of Personality from Select-In and Select-Out Perspectives," *Journal of Applied Psychology*, Vol., 88, 2003, pp. 348–355.

Mumford, M. D., K. Yarkin-Levin, A. L. Korotkin, M. R. Wallis, and J. Marshall-Miles, *Characteristics Relevant to Performance as an Army Leader: Knowledge, Skills, Abilities, Other Characteristics, and Generic Skills*, ARI Research Note 86-24, U.S. Army Research Institute for the Behavioral and Social Sciences, February 1986.

Mumford, M. D., S. J. Zaccaro, F. D. Harding, J. T. Owens, and E. A. Fleishman, "Leadership Skills for a Changing World: Solving Complex Social Problems," *Leadership Quarterly*, Vol. 11, No. 1, 2000, pp. 11-35.

Mumford, T. V., M. A. Campion, F. P. Morgeson, "The Leadership Skills Strataplex: Leadership Skill Requirements Across Organizational Levels," *The Leadership Quarterly*, Vol. 18, 2007, pp. 154–166.

Murphy, K. R., and J. Cleveland, *Understanding Performance Appraisal: Social, Organizational, and Goal-based Perspectives*, Thousand Oaks, Calif.: Sage Publications, 1995.

Newman, Daniel, Ted Kinney, and James L. Farr, "Job Performance Ratings," *Comprehensive Handbook of Psychological Assessment*, Vol. 4, 2004, pp. 373–389.

Occupational Information Network website, undated. As of DATED ACCESSED FOR RESEARCH:
http://www.onetcenter.org/guides.html

Office of Personnel Management, *Assessment Decision Guide*, undated. As of DATE ACCESSED FOR RESEARCH:
http://apps.opm.gov/ADT/Content.aspx?page=TOC

Ones, D. S., S. Dilchert, C. Viswesvaran, and T. A. Judge, "In Support of Personality Assessment in Organizational Settings," *Personnel Psychology*, Vol. 60, No. 4, 2007, pp. 995–1027.

Ones, D. S., and C. Viswesvaran, "A Research Note on the Incremental Validity of Job Knowledge and Integrity Tests for Predicting Maximal Performance," *Human Performance*, Vol. 20, 2007, pp. 293–303.

Oppler, Scott H., Rodney A. McCloy, and John P. Campbell, "The Prediction of Supervisory and Leadership Performance," in John P. Campbell and Deirdre J. Knapp, eds. *Exploring the*

Limits in Personnel Selection and Classification, Mahwah, N.J.: Lawrence Erlbaum Associates, 2001, pp. 389–409.

Pfeffer, J., and R. I. Sutton, "Evidence-Based Management," *Harvard Business Review,* 2006a, pp. 2–13.

Pfeffer, J., and R. I. Sutton, *Hard Facts, Dangerous Half Truths and Total Nonsense: Profiting from Evidence-Based Management,* Boston: Harvard Business Review Press, 2006b.

Quiñones, M. A., J. K. Ford, and M. S. Teachout, "The Relationship Between Work Experience and Job Performance: A Conceptual and Meta-Analytic Review," *Personnel Psychology*, Vol. 48, No. 4, 1995, pp. 887–910.

Ridgeway, Greg, *Generalized Boosted Models: A Guide to the GMB Package*, September 21, 2009. As of February 25, 2013:
https://r-forge.r-project.org/scm/viewvc.php/*checkout*/pkg/inst/doc/gbm.pdf?root=gbm&revision=18&content-type=text%2Fplain&pathrev=18

Roch, S. G., D. J. Woehr, V. Mishra, and U. Kieszczynska, "Rater Training Revisited: An Updated Meta-Analytic Review of Frame-of-Reference Training," *Journal of Occupational and Organizational Psychology*, Vol. 85, No. 2, 2012, pp. 370–395.

Roth, P., P. Bobko, L. McFarland, and M. Buster, "Work Sample Tests in Personnel Selection: A Meta-Analysis of Black-White Differences in Overall and Exercise Scores," *Personnel Psychology*, Vol. 61, 2008, pp. 637–661.

Sackett, P. R. and H. Yang, "Correction for Range Restriction: An Expanded Typology," *Journal of Applied Psychology*, Vol. 85, 2000, No. 1, pp 112–118.

Schiefer, Michael, Albert A. Robbert, John S. Crown, Thomas Manacapilli, and Carolyn Wong, *The Weighted Airman Promotion System: Standardizing Test Scores*, Santa Monica, Calif.: RAND Corporation, MG-678-AF, 2008. As of February 25, 2013:
http://www.rand.org/pubs/monographs/MG678.html

Schmidt, F. L., and J. E. Hunter, "The Validity and Utility of Selection Methods in Personnel Psychology: Practical and Theoretical Implications of 85 Years of Research Findings," *Psychological Bulletin*, Vol. 124, No. 2, 1998, pp. 262–274.

Schmidt, F. L., A. N. Outerbridge, J. E. Hunter, and S. Goff, "Joint Relation of Experience and Ability with Job-Performance—Test of 3 Hypotheses," *Journal of Applied Psychology*, Vol. 73, No. 1, 1988, pp. 46–57.

Schmidt, F. L., and R. D. Zimmerman, "A Counterintuitive Hypothesis About Employment Interview Validity and Some Supporting Evidence," *Journal of Applied Psychology*, Vol. 89, 2004, pp. 553–561.

Shore, C. Wayne, and R. Bruce Gould, *Revalidation of WAPS and SNCOPP, Volume 1: Background, Procedure, and Statistical Results*, Operational Technologies Corporation, October 2004.

SIOP—*See* Society for Industrial and Organizational Psychology, Inc.

Society for Industrial and Organizational Psychology, Inc., *Principles for the Validation and Use of Personnel Selection Procedures,* fourth edition, 2003. As of February 25, 2013: http://www.siop.org/_principles/principles.pdf

Sturman, M. C., "Searching for the Inverted U-shaped Relationship Between Time and Performance: Meta-Analyses of the Experience/Performance, Tenure/Performance, and Age/Performance Relationships," *Journal of Management*, Vol. 29, No. 5, 2003, pp. 609–640.

Taylor, P. J., and B. Small, "Asking Applicants What They Would Do Versus What They Did Do: A Meta-Analytic Comparison of Situational and Past Behaviour Employment Interview Questions," *Journal of Occupational and Organizational Psychology*, Vol. 75, 2002, pp. 277–294.

Tupes, E. C., and R. E. Christal, *Recurrent Personality Factors Based on Trait Ratings*, Lackland Air Force Base, Texas: Aeronautical Systems Division, Personnel Laboratory, Technical Report TR-61-97, 1961.

USAF—*See* U.S. Air Force.

U.S. Air Force, *Military Promotion and Demotion*, Air Force Policy Directive 36-25, June 21, 1993.

———, *Leadership and Force Development*, Air Force Doctrine Document 1-1, February 18, 2006.

———, *The Enlisted Force Structure*, Air Force Instruction 36-2618, February 27, 2009a.

———, *Professional Development Guide*, Air Force Pamphlet 36-2241, July 1, 2009b.

———, *Airman Promotion/Demotion Programs*, Air Force Instruction 36-2502, December 31, 2009c.

———, *Officer and Enlisted Evaluation Systems*, Air Force Instruction 36-2406, October 11, 2011.

Van Iddekinge, C. H., G. R. Ferris, and T. S. Heffner, "Test of a Multistage Model of Distal and Proximal Antecedents of Leader Performance," *Personnel Psychology*, Vol. 62, No. 3, 2009, pp. 463–495.

White, L. A., M. C. Young, A. E. Hunter, and M. G. Rumsey, "Lessons Learned in Transitioning Personality Measures From Research to Operational Settings," *Industrial and Organizational Psychology-Perspectives on Science and Practice*, Vol. 1, 2008, pp. 291–295.

Wiesner, W. H., and S. F. Cronshaw, "A Meta-Analytic Investigation of the Impact of Interview Format and Degree of Structure on the Validity of the Employment Interview," *Journal of Occupational Psychology*, Vol. 61, 1988, pp. 275–290.

Wisecarver, M., R. Schneider, H. Foldes, M. Cullen, *Knowledge, Skills, and Abilities for Military Leader Influence*, Technical Report 1281, U.S. Army Research Institute for the Behavioral and Social Sciences, March 2011.

Yukl, G., *Leadership in Organizations*, Upper Saddle River, N.J.: Prentice Hall, 2006.

Zaccaro, S. J., Trait-based Perspectives of Leadership, *American Psychologist*, Vol. 62, 2007, pp. 6–16.

Zaccaro, S. J., C. Kemp, and P. Bader, "Leader Traits and Attributes," in J. Antonakis, A. T. Cianciolo, and R. J. Sternberg, eds., *The Nature of Leadership*, Thousand Oaks, Calif.: Sage Publications, 2004, pp. 101–124.